EXACTITUDE

EXACTITUDE

On Precision and Play in Contemporary Architecture

Edited by
Pari Riahi
Laure Katsaros
Michael T. Davis

University of Massachusetts Press
AMHERST AND BOSTON

Copyright © 2022 by University of Massachusetts Press
All rights reserved
Printed in the United States of America

ISBN 978-1-62534-671-1 (paper); 672-8 (hardcover)

Designed by Sally Nichols
Set in Bebas Neue and Minion Pro
Printed and bound by Books International, Inc.

Cover design by Sally Nichols
Cover photo: *Triangle Stack One*. Courtesy of LOT-EK.

Library of Congress Cataloging-in-Publication Data
A catalog record for this book is available from Library of Congress

British Library Cataloguing-in-Publication Data
A catalog record for this book is available from the British Library.

Contents

EXACTITUDE AT PLAY

EXACTITUDE AND ITS DISCONTENTS

Acknowledgments

This book is the result of a collaboration between the University of Massachusetts at Amherst, Amherst College, and Mount Holyoke College. The symposium was generously supported by the Department of Architecture at the University of Massachusetts and a Conference Grant from the College of Humanities and Fine Arts. The Five College Consortium Symposium Fund, the Joan Goldstein Spiro '54 Fund of the Department of Art History and Architectural Studies at Mount Holyoke College, the Art and History of Art Department at Amherst College, and the Five College Architectural Studies program supported the symposium as well. Additionally, this volume was supported by the Publication Subvention Fund of the College of Humanities and Fine Arts at the University of Massachusetts and the Faculty Research and Travel Fund at Amherst College.

We are indebted to the following individuals for their meaningful contributions to this collaborative project.

Julie Hayes, Barbara Krauthamer, Joye Bowman, Stephen Schreiber, Nicola Courtright, and Raymond Rennard lent their support and encouragement to the symposium in spite of the multiple uncertainties we faced during this difficult year. We are grateful to them for their faith in this project.

Andee Brown Tetro, Matt Harrington, Lynne Latham, Julie Sarsynski, and Rebecca Thomas made sure that the symposium unfolded flawlessly from the preparatory stages to the final panel. We cannot thank them enough.

Caryn Brause, Gülru Çakmak, Naomi Darling, Marco Monoc, Eldra Dominique Walker, and Erika Zekos were some of the friends and colleagues who offered insight or encouragement for this project at various times.

Ayano Kataoka and Sophie Schilling gracefully animated the virtual space of the symposium with their art, making us collectively present with their memorable performances.

At the University of Massachusetts Press, Mary Dougherty has been an indispensable partner in the process of turning thoughts and ideas into the present volume with care and generosity. We are grateful to Rachel DeShano for her work in the production of this volume, and to Ivo Farvashi, who read the manuscript with exacting editorial care.

EXACTITUDE

Prologue

Pari Riahi, Laure Katsaros, and Michael Davis

Obscure texts by dead people . . . brought me here, to this page, to tell you
everything you will never know.
—Ocean Vuong, *On Earth We're Briefly Gorgeous*

I think we are always searching for something hidden or merely potential
or hypothetical, following its traces whenever they appear on the surface. . . .
The word connects the visible trace with the invisible thing, the absent
thing, the thing that is desired or feared, like an emergency bridge thrown
over the abyss.
—Italo Calvino, *Six Memos for the Next Millennium*

Exactitude is a constitutive element of design and construction, where even the smallest errors may have catastrophic consequences. It involves strict adherence to preestablished
norms, close attention to detail, and a precise transfer of ideas from
their most abstract to their most concrete forms. In spite of its cardinal importance, exactitude is often taken for granted, or overlooked.
One of the key principles of classical and modernist aesthetics,
defined by Leon Battista Alberti with his concept of *lineamenti,*
praised by the Abbé Laugier in the eighteenth century, and by
Le Corbusier in the twentieth, exactitude connotes a totalizing geometrical order that seems at odds with the contemporary trend
toward vernacular architecture, organic forms, and asymmetrical
designs. However, curvilinear, gravity-defying buildings are precisely
the ones that require the greatest degree of computational precision.

This volume seeks to bring the topic of exactitude to the forefront of contemporary debates on architecture, in light of the increasing demand for precision in design and the extraordinary degree of accuracy made possible by new tools and machines. Although new digital technologies have expanded the field of possibilities available to the discipline of architecture in ways that would have been unthinkable a few decades ago, these technological advances have not resulted in the emergence of a distinctive theoretical frameworks. The essays collected here investigate this gap, as they look into current debates about architecture as *techne* and *poiesis*— technological craft and artistic creation. Twenty years into the new millennium, we are still searching for a path forward. The eleven leading theoreticians, architects, and scholars who participated in the symposium we convened at the University of Massachusetts at Amherst in October 2020 provided a platform to engage with the theory and practice of exactitude. In order to see into the future, we turned to the past for clarity and insight. We found our inspiration in a beloved book, Italo Calvino's *Six Memos for the Next Millennium*, a collection of lectures written in 1985 and published posthumously in 1988.[1]

Like the classics to which Calvino devoted another celebrated study, the *Memos* can be read and reread from a multiplicity of perspectives.[2] Drawing from a wide range of literary and philosophical sources, from Ovid to Paul Valéry, Ludwig Wittgenstein, and William Carlos Williams, Calvino offers us insights into the writing process and enumerates the qualities he views as essential to literature. Such qualities, in his opinion, transcend time and place, bridging the gap between past, present, and future. Standing on the threshold of the postindustrial era, Calvino did not venture any guesses about the future of the book as a cultural and technical artifact; nonetheless, he believed that great literature would continue to reflect and incorporate the values he treasured. The cardinal literary values listed by Calvino are lightness, quickness, exactitude, visibility, and multiplicity (because of Calvino's premature death in 1985, a sixth lecture on consistency was never written). Three of these values emerge as particularly relevant for the discipline of architecture: exactitude, multiplicity, and quickness. The first, exactitude, resonates with the creative power of architecture and celebrates the processes that can propel it forward in an ever-shifting landscape. After all, architecture is a journey in which the many facets of exactitude are explored through ideas, transformed into drawings, and executed as artifacts.

Architecture today is being driven by five key factors: stringent regulations at local, national, and global scales that control the parameters of what is possible; a built environment that needs extensive reconfiguring and reuse more than it needs new buildings; novel and complex construction techniques; an array of digital media that have dramatically shifted established norms of thought and action; and, lastly, a host of man-made environmental crises that affect the entire planet, the latest one being climate change. The essays gathered here under the title *Exactitude* reassess the potential of architecture to reorient imagination and creativity in light of rapidly changing conditions in the field. They define architecture as a technically precise act, on the one hand, and as an exercise in perception attuned to a much larger context, on the other. We asked our contributors the following questions: How can architecture reconcile the continuous demand for greater exactitude at the formal, spatial, phenomenal, and tectonic levels, its ethical obligations, and its imaginative capacities? How can recent developments in the field activate the architect's ability to invent new images, concepts, and ideas? Is it still possible for the architect to be defined as an individual with a "signature style" when the medium involves so many layers of technology and collaborative work? Ultimately, how can today's challenges contribute to the development of a new language of architecture that would combine poetic imagination, meaningful action, and a sustainable practice?

Distancing itself from the themes that have been in the forefront of architectural scholarship in the past twenty years (such as sustainability, performance, and formal innovation), this book pursues a longer narrative arc that explores architecture's creative power through its engagement with exactitude. The topic of exactitude invites us to reconsider a discipline divided between technophilia and technophobia; confronted with escalating demands for precision, production, and consumption; and mired in issues of agency and authorship while simultaneously mandated to meet countless ethical and aesthetic needs. Reflecting a genuine desire to bring theory and practice closer, this collection of essays includes the voices of theorists, historians, editors, architects, and writers. While in recent years, conversations about architecture have often led to the formation of isolated thought clusters, the idea of convening theoreticians and practitioners of architecture around this theme aims to open up new avenues for cross-disciplinary thought and creation.

When we organized the Five-College Architecture Symposium on exactitude, our intention was to offer a variety of disciplinary perspectives and to confront radically opposed viewpoints in each panel. On the first day of the colloquium, we paired Christopher Benfey's literary and humanist lecture on architecture and the weather with Alejandro Zaera-Polo's provocative ode to "nonhuman" design, while Mark Wigley provided an essential overview of the fetishization of exactitude in Western architectural theory and practice. We juxtaposed Eric Höweler's account of the paramount importance of technical accuracy in the public monuments he has co-designed with Francesca Hughes's radical critique of the "Filthy Logics" of precision-driven design. The second day of the colloquium expanded the discussion of technology in architecture with presentations on artificial intelligence by Antoine Picon paired with an account of the artistic subversion of machines and industrial objects by Alicia Imperiale. Sunil Bald's manifesto championed a floating architecture, while LOT-EK explored constant reconfiguration(s) of an industrial object into habitable spaces. Teresa Stoppani's poetic meditation took us for a spiraling promenade through literary and architectural texts in search of the in-exact. Finally, the roundtable moderated by Cynthia Davidson offered play as an antidote to exactitude.

The structure of the present volume differs from the logic of the colloquium: built around commonalities rather than differences, each section brings together architects and theoreticians who either cleave to exactitude or express a predilection for the inexact. Although we had to sacrifice some of the creative tensions that resulted from the confrontation of starkly opposing viewpoints in the colloquium format, we privileged clarity and legibility, while preserving the interdisciplinarity that is essential to our project. The essays in this volume offer varied and even contradictory accounts of exactitude, but the friction between them presents new possibilities for creative practice and critical thought. As a collection, they delineate what an architecture of the exact may be, and what defines its opposite, the in-exact in architecture.

If exactitude is the overarching principle that governs architecture, how do architects respond to its relentless demand, read intolerance? If we are to equate the act of building with erring, Stanley Tigerman has suggested, since all built form is "a provisional approximation of concepts," the question arises of how to position one's practice in the center of these "approximations [which] are rife with errors."[3] In the opening section, "Exactitude, or the Art of Intolerance," we acknowledge the power of exactitude, its reach and its domain. In juxtaposing Mark Wigley's examination of historical definitions of exactitude in architecture, beginning with Le Corbusier and going back to Alberti, with the practices of Alejandro Zaera-Polo and Eric Höweler, we focus on how exactitude shapes the architect's projects and worldviews.

Mark Wigley explores how the quest for exactitude, understood as a desire for perfection, control, and order, has shrouded buildings in what he calls "vast icebergs of data." In his view, the relentless move toward digital precision and the speed with which data are loaded and consumed presents a dilemma: architectural artifacts that encourage the slowing down of movement while also continuously changing in almost imperceptible flows are subjected to innumerable data sets. Wigley reminds us that the demand for ever-increasing precision in architectural design is not simply the defining trait of our technologically obsessed era. He carefully traces the lineage of exactitude to modern architects and in particular to Le Corbusier. Wigley maps out Corbusier's "voyages of discovery into exactitude" from his study of the Parthenon to his own Villa Savoye, where the display of exactitude creates a meditative space. He further asserts that Le Corbusier's love of exactitude was embedded in "sensuality, desire and emotion." By unpacking the contradictions of mastering exactitude in order to surpass it, Wigley claims that for Le Corbusier, architecture could emerge only from exactitude, not only by being made exact but also by manifesting its exactitude. Wigley then leads us toward tolerance, the counterpoint that, in his view, is as essential as exactitude, arguing that buildings are a sum total of many "nested" tolerances, concealed by architecture to "sustain the illusion of the static object."

   Alejandro Zaera-Polo's "New Narratives in the After-Post-Truth Age: Posthumanism, Precision, and Conservation" identifies the COVID-19 pandemic as the brutal face of climate change and environmental degradation, and muses on how current and upcoming crises that will shape the built environment stem from "nonhuman processes and populations." Criticizing what he views as the current stagnation in the architectural field, he argues for a radical change in the discipline. Championing a precise, data-oriented approach to architecture in contrast to the view of Francesca Hughes, Zaera-Polo places exactitude at the core of his practice. He invites us to go back to the drawing board, mindful of climatic crises and of global and local forces, which, he suggests, will make architecture more accountable, responsive, and innovative. Departing from Mark Wigley's path toward tolerance, he calls for an architecture that focuses on "intolerances," preoccupied with the physical and quantitative characteristics of the building and its environment. Zaera-Polo contends that this "intolerant architecture," strictly based on environmental, material, and scientific data, is our only way out of the current crisis. In his view, the search for quantification and measurability will be creative, although its factual basis will set limits to its reach. Zaera-Polo's definition of exactitude as a force to be reckoned with—a core value that orients architecture at a time of crisis—is complex and provocative.

   Eric Höweler's essay, "Verify in Field," introduces us to an architectural practice that distinguishes itself through its technical exactitude while addressing larger societal issues, such as the memorialization of traumatic events in American history. Exploring projects developed by their architectural firm, H+Y, Höweler provides insights into the technical aspects of design, from fabrication to construction and verification on site. To use Calvino's words, he shows how architecture connects the "visible trace" embodied in a memorial with "the invisible thing, the absent thing" that it strives to represent, namely, historical trauma. Höweler elaborates how "verify in field," a conventional notation that accounts for the space between the idea and the physical artifact, answers Zaera-Polo's provocation to go beyond the representational. In Höweler's projects, such as the Sean Collier Memorial on the MIT campus in Cambridge, Massachusetts (2015), one finds a return to the marvel and anxiety of construction that resonates with medieval and early modern architectural endeavors. However, in contrast to historical practices, new technologies continue to upend the established sequence of ideation to realization. Today's drawings, Zaera-Polo points out, "are not drawings at all" but fabrication tools. Nevertheless, technical details such as the wear of a saw on the stones of an arch introduce variables that force architects to mind the gap between model and structure. By focusing on construction, Höweler argues that architects can reclaim their agency and assume more responsibility as they engage with the material and cultural facets of a project from a new perspective.

Ironically, but not unexpectedly, any attempt to define exactitude brings us face-to-face with the forces that oppose or counter it. Paul Emmons astutely recognized the tension between the genuine "desire to see a future building in design drawings" and the "far more fluid and wooly process of adaptations" that is part of any project's realization.[4] Addressing this tension has led many architects to engage with the process of adapting and translating their ideas and drawings, taking into account the many conditions that influence them. These thoughts activate "Exactitude Adrift," where Christopher Benfey's essay "Exactitude and the Weather" and Sunil Bald's "Building in the Floating World" focus on the external forces that work against exactitude in architecture, such as the weather, or a shifting cultural environment that inspires the architect to let go of rigid norms and boundaries.

As he considers what might oppose or hinder exactitude, Christopher Benfey identifies the weather as a force that continuously challenges architecture, forcing it to exist in time and to adapt to climatic conditions. He suggests that architecture historically arose in opposition to the weather as a means to shelter and protect humans against the violent forces of nature. By referring to the Japanese aesthetics of wabi-sabi and the Romantics' penchant for ruins, he invites us to think of a more nimble, open, and accepting architecture, attuned to weather and its unpredictability. Through material and literary examples, Benfey shows us how the search for exactitude often musters up its opposite, the effect of time and weather. Conjuring up Eupalinos, Paul Valéry's imaginary architect, Benfey suggests that an architecture of exactitude might fulfill its mandate by becoming as diaphanous, transient, and ever-changing as the weather itself.

Sunil Bald defines exactitude through floating, making a case for the unpredictable events and collaborative processes that informed the practice he cofounded, studioSUMO, to complete a series of projects for Josai University in Sakado, Satama, Japan. Turning to Eastern philosophies, and in particular to Japanese art and literature, Bald reminds us of the power of being unmoored, outside, and foreign. Unforeseen circumstances, events, objects, and people (read collaborators, inhabitants, clients, and communities) affect the space of ideation, pulling some threads, and pushing others. Bald highlights the critical space that lies, often dormant and invisible, between the precision of the drawn idea and the physical attributes of the finished product. Working on projects for Josai University, Bald found strength in the displacement outside of accustomed environmental, cultural, and disciplinary norms. Answering Zaera-Polo's call to embrace foreignness as a weapon for the architect rather than an obstacle, Bald reminds us of the importance of context, with all its shifting complexities, in bringing the project of architecture to the point of exactitude.

Ever since the Industrial Revolution, machines, ever more intelligent, precise, complex, and confounding, have claimed a prominent space in thoughts and actions as they pertain to architecture. The idea of subverting or misappropriating the intended use of machines and objects has been present for nearly as long as they have been part of our environment. In the section titled "Exactitude at Play," the many ways in which functional artifacts and machines can spur architectural and artistic imagination are explored by Ada Tolla, Giuseppe Lignano, and Thomas de Monchaux, who explain the creative processes behind LOT-EK's STACK projects, while Alicia Imperiale investigates the "creative misuse" of photocopy machines in Bruno Munari's avant-garde artistic practice.[5]

In their essay "Stacks," Ada Tolla, Giuseppe Lignano, and Thomas de Monchaux elaborate on the creative and practical processes of LOT-EK through a discussion of three different projects. By reappropriating an industrial object, in this case the standard ISO shipping container, they align the process of invention with the roots of the verb *invenire* as the process of stumbling upon a discovery. Reconfiguring the shipping container in architectural terms then becomes an exercise in exactitude: cutting it, arranging it, stacking it, and using specific calculations to redefine the box as an architectural space. Their TRIANGLE STACK ONE is open to the possibility of shared intelligence. Going back and forth between the architects' vision and the foreman's experience, playing on subtle readjustments and embodied intelligence, architecture becomes an act performed in conjunction with others. TRIANGLE STACK TWO explores a quantifiable form of exactitude, with measurements, loads, and water volume, but also calls on the ingenuity of the architect to devise the joint and elaborate on accommodating displacement. In that project and in their practice, LOT-EK extends the realm of possibilities, walking a fine line between structural feasibility and playfulness. The third and last project discussed in the essay, DRIVELINES STUDIOS, builds upon the discoveries of the first two to deploy a systematic approach that resolves program, structure, and enclosure in the context of permanent buildings. LOT-EK's work makes the "imaginative action" the primary task of the architect, constantly corroborating productive and practical realities with imaginative intuitions.

Alicia Imperiale's "Machine Consequences" discusses the hacking of machines, in particular the Xerox machine, by the artist Bruno Munari as "creative misuse." She suggests that such endeavors, which challenge the direct lineage from code to matter, and instead open the door for "messiness" and other material explorations, may be a way to engage with new technologies. Imperiale explores the playful ways in which Munari tampered with the photocopying process to subvert and expand the definition of art in the 1960s. Although the once ubiquitous Xerox machine is almost a relic nowadays, Munari's engagement with technology prefigures critical levels of operation that relate to digital fabrication in today's architectural practice. Imperiale suggests that Johan Huizinga's *Homo Ludens* (1938), which developed the notion of play as the "enactment of the inexact," is instrumental in engaging with the uncertainty at work in a seemingly predictable process. She argues that engaging with chance was liberating for Munari, as it opened up the political and operational potential embedded in this continuum. In the same spirit as LOT-EK's stacked shipping containers, Munari's work is both precise and playful, highly structured and yet utterly unforeseeable, open to variables and happenstance. This experimental approach elevates exactitude from a numeric and quantifiable procedure to what Imperiale refers to as a "progressional procedure" dictated by variation and change.

But what if we could will another kind of exactitude into being? Rather than statistics, numbers, and data, it would lead us to a discovery of objects, elements, buildings, and cities summed up by complex sensory memories that defy clear categories. Mhairi McVicar proposes that "precise intentions do not guarantee certainty" and offers that architecture finds its force in the details, "pursued through uncertainty and ambiguity incurred by planned and unplanned deviations," which are at every point "negotiated with precision."[6] In the section "Exactitude and Its Discontents," Francesca Hughes's "Filthy Logics: Exactitude and the Architecture of Mediocrity" and Teresa Stoppani's "The In-Exact Words of Architecture" take issue with the contemporary fetishization of precision and certainty. Hughes uncovers the connection between the emergence of statistics as a scientific discipline and today's worship of big data, while Stoppani offers a learned meditation on the city as a collection of literary and philosophical fragments—the remains of exactitude.

Francesca Hughes dives into pointlessness in reaction to the "neoliberal filth" that, in her view, has taken over the field of architecture in our era. Questioning the reign of nineteenth-century statistics and its contemporary counterpart, big data, she posits that their seemingly inevitable alliance is only a fabrication, which we have embraced far too uncritically. Going back to the mathematician and sociologist Adolphe Quetelet (1796–1874), who was instrumental in constructing a "fundamental filthy logic" to predict human behavior, Hughes explores how statistical laws became "objective knowledge" and reminds us that predictability is always mitigated by the use of scale. Probing the "exactitude of the inexact," that of data and machine, Hughes confirms that our actions in contemporary practice, comprised of continuous chains of decision making, are engineered into processes that are deeply rooted in the statistical logics and theories of the nineteenth century. Oscillating between Samuel Beckett's words and Quetelet's bell curve, she reminds us how any practice that is based on measure and exactitude also presents itself as an aesthetic project.

Teresa Stoppani investigates exactitude in the textual and urban realms by first focusing on inexactitude. Inviting the reader to embark on an interpretive journey, a hypothetical meandering through texts and images of the city, she considers the importance of opening up a space for a questioning, a "what if," which in turn will be the harbinger of change. Stoppani emphasizes that exactitude's deep connections to the vague and indefinite opens up architecture, both as a discipline in a state of perpetual change and as an edifice to be inhabited and maintained. As she weaves together meticulously chosen fragments from Italo Calvino, Roland Barthes, Antoine-Chrysostome Quatremère de Quincy, Lieven De Boeck, Giovanni Battista Piranesi, Massimo Cacciari, Saskia Sassen, and Sanford Kwinter, images of the city form and disintegrate, turning the experience of the essay into an interpretive performance and an act of meditation.

Finally, Cynthia Davidson's postlude connects the theme of the symposium with the virtual format in which it unfolded as a result of the COVID-19 pandemic. Emphasizing the strangeness of two-dimensional, noiseless, and precisely calibrated conversations held over Zoom for an invisible audience, her essay reintroduces sounds and bodies into our narrative of exactitude through the disruptive and energizing force of laughter.

Our work around the theme of exactitude is finished, and yet it feels as if it were only beginning. Over the course of the colloquium and the conversations that followed, as spoken words solidified into written text, different aspects of exactitude emerged: suggestive, generative, obsessive, even oppressive. If there is any conclusion to draw, or any hint to be given in this prelude, it is the certainty that the fate of architecture is intertwined with exactitude, which may either help or hinder, open up or shut down the space of creativity. Although the term "exactitude" suggests a strict adherence to mathematical and linguistic norms, which leaves no space for error, uncertainty, or flaws, our search has taken us in the opposite direction. Instead of inhibiting creation, or restricting the scope of architecture to technical accuracy, exactitude has the power to generate its many opposites: fluidity, openness, tolerance, and playfulness. Viewed as a whole, the essays gathered in this volume confirm our original intuition, that precision and imagination are allies, not enemies. It is our hope that new directions for architectural theory and practice may emerge from this constellation of voices. Borrowing Ocean Vuong's words again, "If we are lucky, the end of the sentence is where we might begin."[7]

NOTES

1 "Exactitude," *Six Memos for the Next Millennium,* trans. Patrick Creagh (Cambridge, MA: Harvard University Press, 1988).

2 Italo Calvino, *Why Read the Classics,* trans. Martin McLaughlin (New York: Vintage, 2001). An excerpt from *Why Read the Classics* translated by Patrick Creagh first appeared in the *New York Review of Books* in October 1986.

3 Tigerman identifies ten contaminants as the sources of either error or certitude in architecture: congestion, death, dimensionality, gravity, indeterminacy, mimesis, nostalgia, otherness, stasis, and synthesis. Stanley Tigerman, "Apophasis, Wabi-Sabi, and the Ethics of Errancy," in *Error, Perspecta: The Yale Architectural Journal* 46 (New Haven, CT: Yale University Press, 2013), 192.

4 Paul Emmons, *Drawing Imagining Building: Embodiment in Architectural Design Practices* (Abingdon, UK: Routledge, 2019), 204.

5 Another panelist, Antoine Picon, gave a presentation at the symposium "Humans, Artificial Intelligence and the Future of Design" that echoed some of the themes discussed by Imperiale and LOT-EK. Picon observed that while humans occupy a central position in the architectural equation through the capacity to choose among the ranges of options and solutions proposed by machines, machines may be able to update "powerful mythical forces" by following rules other than our own. His presentation suggested that automation, animation, and artificial intelligence may work to perturb the exactitude of design by producing glitches and imperfections that, in the end, open the way to a new poetics of human presence.

6 Mhairi McVicar, *Precision in Architecture: Certainty, Ambiguity, and Deviation* (Abingdon, UK: Routledge, 2019), 240.

7 Ocean Vuong, *On Earth We're Briefly Gorgeous* (New York: Penguin Press, 2019), 10.

EXACTITUDE, OR THE ART OF INTOLERANCE

Chapter 1
The Intolerances of Architecture

Mark Wigley

There is much talk of exactitude in architecture today. All the thousands of elements assembled in even the simplest building are defined by ever more precise computation in design, modeling, analysis, testing, selection, sourcing, budgeting, specification, fabrication, transportation, assembly, installation, fastening, monitoring, maintenance, and representation. It is as if architecture itself is now suspended in clouds of digital precision. Or, to say it the other way round, buildings have become the visible tip of vast icebergs of data. It is not just a matter of the countless calculations leading to a building but the building itself as a site of continuous calculations in a thoroughly electronic life. Buildings are produced and lived electronically.

Yet architecture is a relatively low-technology field. It is hard to find a lower one. Cooking, for example, is much more advanced, as even modest kitchens have become experimental chemical and biological laboratories. Perhaps we should be proud of how low and slow architecture unfolds in an accelerating world. Or at least appreciate that architecture might be a form of resistance to the environment around it—never simply slow but a gesture of slowing. Even then, the smallest, simplest, and slowest building has countless parts made of countless materials coming from countless places to form what appears to be a single contained, impervious and immobile object but is more like a set of valves attached to multiple infrastructures ranging across local, regional, continental, and planetary scales—interplanetary even, if you consider the continuous intimate exchanges between buildings and satellites. The seemingly solid object is actually a set of hidden openings that hosts overlapping, interacting, and ever transforming communities of people, other animals, insects, plants, microbes, chemistries, technologies, and electromagnetic waves.

Buildings host movement by not moving, standing still so that everything else can move through them. They don't flow precisely because flow is what they are about, in the sense that the static, clearly defined geometry of a swimming pool makes liquid play possible and even magnifies the sense of liquidity that it hosts by resolutely not participating in that liquidity. Seemingly simple immobile buildings are actually complex movement systems. Rooms are eddies, the swirling of multiple intersecting currents. If movement is by definition relative, the building hosts movement by repressing its own movements and all the movements that sustain it. After all, even the seemingly impervious structure defining a space is infused with the constant hidden motion of air, water, gas, and electricity flowing through hidden webs of intricately folded tubes, pipes, and wires. The temperature, moisture, stiffness, and dimensions of all the elements and cavities perpetually flux. A structure is never as static as it appears. Buildings discretely vibrate, pulsate, flex, warp, dilate, breathe, and sweat.

The visual singularity and stability of a building and its spaces are, as it were, a foil to all the countless flows that it facilitates, accommodates, absorbs, channels, filters, or resists. The appearance that the building itself doesn't flow, reinforced by hiding the internal flows that sustain it, is a calculated effect—perhaps even the crucial effect. Architecture is a particular repression of movement, a self-disciplining, like a ballet pose that requires huge internal forces working against each other in the muscles and tendons to produce the effect of a floating stillness. Architecture is the art of standing still in a world that is a world only inasmuch as it is on the move.

Contemporary discourse casts all of this in terms of computation as each dimension becomes more precise and new dimensions keep getting added. Every month there seems to be a new way to measure and thereby rethink and remake architecture. The apparent stillness of architecture is surrounded by a constant flurry of new protocols for more precisely monitoring an ever larger and more diverse set of variables. But discourse about computation in architecture and architecture in computation—which celebrates its own progressiveness and contemporaneity—faithfully, albeit unwittingly, echoes the discourse about exactitude made by architects in the early twentieth century. The focus has shifted from industrialization and standardization to customization, responsiveness, performance, and interactivity. Yet it is ultimately an expansion of the zone of exactitude rather than a transformation.

Architecture, Exactly

Take Le Corbusier, far and away the most influential polemicist of the last century. Like so many colleagues, he wanted the new precision of industrial techniques and science to reshape architecture. Modern architecture would be something exact. It would even be incubated within the space of calculation, pulled into the present by precision. Yet the very timeliness of exactitude paradoxically unites the newest designs with the timeless architecture of the past:

> Precision reigns.
> Economy leads.
> We are pulled invincibly on a new axis.
> Another era has begun.
> In the pure atmosphere of calculation we find again certain spirit of clarity that animated the immortal past.[1]

It isn't simply that architecture should be industrialized like any other object as a more efficient instrument to support a more efficient life. Recalibrated architecture will in turn be crucial to systems of industrialization—feeding and upgrading the networks that nurture it. Exactitude is a crucial symptom of a modern architecture, which is to say an architecture synchronized to its time, but also an effect of that architecture. In other words, architecture would both benefit from the progress of exactitude and contribute to that progress. In the end, it is not simply a question of making architecture more exact but of recognizing the architecture within exactitude itself. Modern architecture will be found in the exact rather than invented. It is exacted from the exact.

Le Corbusier loved the word "exact," relishing any opportunity to use it. "Exactitude" was an especially exciting word, even erotically charged. After all, the whole obsession with exactness might be sexual and require a more psychoanalytical and critical analysis. It involves fantasies of control, of controlling and being controlled, constraint and release. The world of calculation is never separate from that of sensuality, desire, and emotion. On the contrary. In fact, the sensuality of exactitude was Le Corbusier's whole point, organizing, for example, *Toward an Architecture* of 1923, arguably the most read manifesto for modern architecture.

A particular theory of exactitude orchestrates the all too familiar book. The argument begins with the assertion that engineers are healthy (physically, aesthetically, and morally), engaged, alive, and leading the way. Architects are unhealthy, detached, dying, and lagging behind. Why is the engineer healthy? He, and it is unambiguously "he," works with economy, calculation, and machines. In other words, "exactitude."[2] Health is exactness. Architects are unhealthy because they lack exactness. But here is the trick. They could wake up and do something the engineers cannot, by turning exactness into art. If a building is an inhabited machine, it becomes architecture only by being more than a machine, more than exact. Yet this extra of art-beauty-sensuality-poetry-emotion-sentiment-thought is somehow made possible by the exacting technical world it transcends. No exactitude means no emotion, which means no architecture. In a certain sense, architects have to pass through exactitude on the way toward something else.

The architect, for example, has to master construction "as exactly as a thinker masters grammar"—following the classical idea of mastery whereby supposedly one can speak grammatically without having a significant thought but not think significantly without correct grammar.[3] Only when the rules have been faithfully and deeply absorbed can they be broken to poetic effect. Freedom of thought and feeling is made possible by exactly following exacting demands with exact instruments. This means obeying the law of economy, which is "pure manifestations of calculation . . . using materials completely and exactly,"[4] in exact response to exact needs, as in the past when houses were made to man's "exact measure."[5] New materials such as concrete and steel offer new "exactitude" since they so "exactly" adapt to theory and calculations.[6] Furthermore, as industry ties humans and machines ever more tightly together, both become more exact. Every worker has to operate with "implacable precision" when every part has to be "exact" to continue "with exactitude" its role as a component in a bigger assemblage.[7]

Human needs are exact, as are the tools, materials, systems, and ideas to address those needs. The scene in which architecture is born, especially the architecture immediately ahead, is made of multiple layers of mutually reinforcing and mutually demanding exactitude. Modern architecture is the art of exactitude, which is not the art of being exact but the art that emerges out of, through, and even away from exactitude.

Voyages into the Exact

This classical yet paradoxical idea of mastering exactitude precisely in order to move beyond it became a formula in so many Le Corbusier texts. Take, for example, the major 1924 lectures on the "new spirit" in architecture that began with the assertion that "precision rules":

> The house has two purposes. First, it is a *machine for living,* that is to say a machine intended to provide us with assistance for speed and exactitude in the work, a diligent and efficient machine to meet the requirements of the body: comfort. But it is then the useful place for meditation, and finally the place where beauty exists and brings to the mind the calm that is indispensable. Everything that concerns the practical purposes of the house, the engineer brings it; as for meditation, the spirit of beauty, the order which reigns (and will be the support of this beauty), it will be *the architecture.* Work of the engineer on the one hand; architecture on the other hand.[8]

The engineer's exacting world of mechanics, speed, and efficiency incubates its apparent opposite: meditation, calm, and beauty. More paradoxical still, exactitude can be left behind only by being entered more deeply. Architects are lovers of exactitude that find a path beyond the exact within the very demands of the exact. To master exactitude is to obey it obsessively—overcoming by obeying. A "great constructive exactitude" and "precision of intention" produce a "pleasure of mathematical order" that releases beauty and emotion as engineering gives way to architecture. It is even as if architects have to go further into the engineers' space of calculation than the engineers in order to transcend that space.

This ever more intense drive for exactitude has itself become the dominant force shaping modern environments, Le Corbusier noted in the 1924 foreword to *Urbanisme:*

> To-day, our enthusiasm is for exactitude. An exactitude carried to its furthest limits and raised to an ideal: the search for perfection.
> This modern sentiment is a spirit of geometry, a spirit of construction and synthesis. Exactitude and order are its essential condition. Our means are such that exactitude and order are within our reach, and the unremitting toil which has given us the means of realization has created in us a sentiment which is an aspiration, an ideal, an unswerving tendency, an imperious need.[9]

If exactitude is a drive, a relentless subordination to needs and means, then each new level of exactness only creates the compulsion toward even greater exactness. In 1934, Le Corbusier insisted, "The construction of the building, which is currently *done to the nearest centimeter,* has to move to the regime of industrial exactitude *to the nearest tenth of a millimeter.*"[10] Architecture is being steadily "led by the path of exactitude" toward that status of "equipment," the efficient world of "exact function" without any waste.

The second edition of the first volume of Le Corbusier's self-congratulatory *Oeuvre complète* even begins with a 1936 letter about the need for architects to make "voyages of discovery" into the "exactitude" and thereby beauty of nature (even in the perfection of natural catastrophes) in order to finally "banish stupidity."[11] Exactitude is never simply an aesthetic. It is rather a philosophical investigation, a questioning rather than an answering, even if certain constants are discovered along the way. Le Corbusier's 1934 preface to the second volume of the *Oeuvre complète,* for example, says his repeated use of the same words is based on having "once and for all, recognized exactitude."[12] After all, prescriptions for architecture have to be as exact as what they describe.

Le Corbusier's attempt to standardize a proportional system in *Le Modulor* in 1950 similarly presented itself as an advance in the history of exactitude in architecture, even a domestication of the exact: "We may safely say that such exactitude, such rigor of mathematics and harmony have never before been applied to that simplest accessory of daily life: the dwelling."[13] The follow-up *Modulor II* of 1955 speaks of exactitude as the source of physical and intellectual comfort, but again also of the "poetic escape" that is art. Exactitude is both the "implacable" law to follow and the means of the greatest release. The ultimate dream of an "ineffable space" that exceeds immediate comprehension and description is based on meticulous calculation. The book speaks of "the spark, the glow, the blaze of light born of exactitude" and concludes its argument with the line "Exactitude, springboard of lyricism."[14] Relentless exactitude launches the human into a world beyond the exact.

Performing Exactness

Le Corbusier constantly locates forms of exactitude and celebrates the exactness of his own thinking and work in response. The narrative is all about exactitude, whether of body functions, sport, science, machine, calculation, economy, industry, construction, or law. The United States, for example, is attractive for being the land of exactitude (as evidenced in skyscrapers, the stock market, jazz, and tap dancing) and therefore a model for the new forms of the exact that could incubate new architecture in the hands of an artist.[15] Exactitude is the engine of modernity. But Le Corbusier equally saw exactitude in classical temples, Japanese woodcuts, medieval cathedrals, and Roman city planning. Architecture was not modern because it was exact. It was architecture only inasmuch as it was exact.

  Modern forms of exactness inevitably incubate a modern architecture even if architects are pathologically slow to recognize it. Architecture is part of the development of exactitude, albeit one of its slowest-moving branches—always catching up to the logic of the "exact sciences," even needing to catch up with itself, or learn from those moments in which it was once at the leading edge. The Parthenon, for example, is a model for the state-of-the-art of exactness liberating sensual, emotional, and intellectual force—technology becoming art. *Towards an Architecture* portrays it as a "machine for stirring emotion" in which "fractions of a millimeter come into play," with the curve of the column "as rational as that of a large artillery shell."[16] Indeed, its exactitude matched twentieth-century ideas about machine precision: "The whole of this plastic mechanics is realized in marble with the rigor we have learned to apply in machines. The impression is one of cut and polished steel."[17] A 1946 essay "Architecture and the Mathematical Spirit" positions this "frightening exactitude" of the Parthenon's machinelike effect within a series of examples (including a Leonardo drawing, a cathedral, and a tree) to demonstrate that "rigor and exactitude" is always the basis of harmony and character.[18] Exactitude is not an option for architects but the very space of architecture.

It was never simply about being exact. Rather, it is a matter of presenting exactness as such. Even the exactitude of the Parthenon is exactly presented: "Everything is stated precisely."[19] Le Corbusier did not just call for modern architecture to be as precise as any other machine, within one-tenth of a millimeter. More importantly, like the Parthenon, it had to flaunt this exactitude—a thoroughly classical ambition.

This was in turn part of an even longer history of exactitude in and as architecture. The 1682 publication of *Les édifices antiques de Rome dessinés et mesurés très exactement* by Antoine Desgodets, who had been one of the first students of the Royal Academy of Architecture, gave the "exact" measurements of the ancient monuments of Rome when "exact" meant 2.25 millimeters.[20] While Desgodets sided with the academy's view that proportions were absolute, his book enabled Claude Perrault to discredit the supposed exactitude of classical proportions. Perrault noted the extraordinary "exactitude" of the human eye in judging beauty.[21] Yet he insisted that what the eye so precisely perceives as beautiful has nothing to do with proportional exactitude.[22] Admired buildings are anyway inexact relative to the original exactitude established by those that invented architecture, even though the "precision and cleanness" of a building's execution was key to its beauty.[23] Perrault sought to give a "new precision" to the supposedly singular and immutable orders that were in practice diverse and changing by standardizing them to the mean of the measures of those buildings the eye judged as beautiful. A new idea of exactitude was used to undermine an older one in the name of science.

One could make a timeline of architects steadily increasing the degree of exactitude demanded of buildings. Buckminster Fuller, for example, in the "Everything that I know" TV recording of 1975, said that his 1953 geodesic aluminum-framed and plastic-skinned dome for the Ford Motor Company had to be built to the tolerance of one ten-thousandth of an inch, like an automobile, rather the typical quarter-of-an-inch tolerance in buildings.[24]

In all these cases, the display of exactitude, which is something very different from being exact, was directly linked to an authoritarian rhetoric of "control," "order," "purity," and "cleanliness." Le Corbusier's *Decorative Art of Today* (1925), for example, explores the way that a sense of exactness occupies the place once given to decoration and ultimately becomes a form of decoration appropriate to its time. A new kind of effect emerges from machines stripped of ornament, a beauty that can even exceed that of nature, since machines can have an exactitude not found in nature.[25] They both do their work "with purity and exactitude" and radiate "an aesthetic of purity, of exactitude."[26] This association of exactitude and purity would become most obvious in Le Corbusier's concept of "exact air" purified of bacteria, excluding threatening microbial others from the interior along with variations of temperature and moisture. An exact environment is both controlled and controlling.

Precision Plaster

This association of exactitude and exclusion is not accidental. Exactitude implies absence of error, aberration, or hybridity. It is explicitly linked to an extractive logic of service-slavery that systematically pushes multiple others out and down. After all, the question of exactitude is really the question of tolerance. Buildings are multiple nested sets of tolerances with an arsenal of materials and techniques that are constantly deployed to conceal any inexactitude of movement that might be revealed in gaps, undulations, leaks, and squeaks. The discipline of architecture is dependent on a whole array of gaskets and caulking to veil tolerances and sustain the illusion of a static object. A large part of the foundational treatises of Vitruvius and Leon Battista Alberti is devoted to the precise production, mixture, and application of successive layers of lime plaster and final polishing to avoid (in Alberti's words) "defects," "gaps," "blemishes," "swellings," "sinkings," "splittings," "warps," or "cracks" to produce "smooth," "square," "level," and "plumb" white surfaces that hold the "beholder's eye" on what is exact. As with Le Corbusier, exactitude of point, line, and surface depended entirely on the ancient craft of stucco. Alberti praised the ancient practice to "make those Parts which lay nearest the Eye as neat and exactly polished as was possible."[27] The outer surfaces are orchestrated and finished to bring the effect of exactness to the eye. Architects are trained in the art of repressing inexactness so that viewers can, as it were, project a sense of exactness into the hidden depths of the object.

It is crucial to remember that the exactness Alberti calls for is an exactness of ornament, a purified and thereby purifying regime of the outer layer:

> For every Thing must be reduced to exact Measure, so that all the Parts may correspond with one another . . . with nothing interfering that may blemish either the Order or the Materials, but every Thing squared to exact Angles and similar Lines.[28]

> In short, let every thing be measured, and put together with the greatest Exactness of Lines and Angles, that the beholder's eye may have a clear and distinct View.[29]

Classical architecture is a system of ornamentation that constructs a sense of exactness beyond it and needs to have the sense of its own exactness maintained by a set of prosthetic techniques for veiling tolerance. Le Corbusier's cult of the exact in the purported absence of ornament depends on the same techniques for allowing but disguising specific degrees of inexactitude.

Tolerance is calculated intolerance—to unwanted movements, bacteria, insects, species, temperatures, smells, and designated others. It is precisely not hospitality. Architecture is even a form of intolerance. For some, it is the very form of intolerance. Or, to say it another way, intolerance always produces an architecture.

The Perfect Stain

Yet it is a mistake to simply counter industrial and now electronic exactitude with appeals to the supposed lost treasures of creativity, imagination, and humanity. The counterdiscourses that accompanied the emergence of modern industrialized architecture as a mode of calculation—and critiqued it by privileging the body, social life, locality, identity, craft, poetry, history, and nature—were actually rival claims on the exact.

Think of John Ruskin. No one was more skeptical of the precision of machines or loved cracks and stains more. The few weeks' delay in publication of first volume of *The Stones of Venice* in March 1851 allowed him to add an appendix condemning the almost completed Crystal Palace for embodying the sacrifice of architecture to mathematical calculation in the age of machines that ruthlessly turns humans into machines. Ruskin condemned the building for the very reasons that most historians of modern architecture would later celebrate it. Again, the complaint was not simply against the look of modernity. Ruskin was even more angry with what he saw as the related contemporary crime of the "exact" restoration of Gothic buildings. To "reproduce with mathematical exactitude" a mutilated building part, as was proudly said of recent restoration work at Chartres Cathedral, was to mutilate the building even more violently.[30] Such exactitude undoing the effects of time was a "cancer" spreading across Gothic architecture.

Yet Ruskin was never simply antiexactitude. During his first extended stay in Venice in 1845, he was desperate after four days of unsuccessfully trying capture the stains and cracks in a rendering of a palazzo facade, considering his drawings "a written note of certain facts" that recorded a disappearing world, including the weeds growing out of the building: "I am thoroughly thrown on my back with the Palazzo Foscari—don't know what the deuce to do with it. I have all its measures and mouldings & that is something, but I can't get on with the general view . . . the beauty of it is in the cracks & and the stains, and to draw these out is impossible and I am in despair."[31]

Ruskin finally solved the problem by buying some daguerre-otypes of the building that "perfectly" rendered all the imperfections, enabling him to get the drawing correct. In other words, he used the precision of a modern machine to guide his hand to capture the world before such machines.

> It is a noble invention, say what they will of it, and any one who has worked and blundered and stammered as I have done for four days, and then sees the thing he has been trying to do so long in vain done perfectly and faultlessly in half a minute, won't abuse it after-wards.
>
> It is very nearly the same as carrying off the palace itself—every chip of stone & stain is there—and, of course, there is no mistake about proportions.[32]

The photograph carries the truth of the building in precisely preserving the chips and stains. It was not by chance that Ruskin claimed to have first discovered architecture on the same trip when attracted to the "close fitting" of stones, the exactness of medieval craft he felt had been lost in the Renaissance use of mechanical modes of production. Ruskin is not opposed to modern techniques simply because they are exact. On the contrary, he is a lover of the forms of exactitude obscured by the latest methods. For Ruskin, a building is different kinds of superimposed precision. He insists that no craftsperson produces work using measurements, and opposes, for example, someone else's "precise" measurements of pottery, talking of his own "much less complex, though even more scrupulous, measurements which I shall require."[33] There is a greater precision to the craft that contemporary calculation cannot reach.

Where Le Corbusier talks of mechanical exactitude and smuggles in feeling, Ruskin talks about feeling and smuggles in exactitude—even talking about an exactitude of feeling: "My life has chanced to be one of gradual progress in the things which I began in childish voice; I can measure with almost mathematical exactitude the degree of feeling with which less and greater degrees of wealth or skill affect my mind."[34] This mathematics of feeling complicates the question of tolerance, which is really the question of intolerance, that shapes architecture and is arguably its central mission.

Clouds, Precisely

In a final twist, the discourse of exactitude can be turned against the very idea of architecture. There are architects who cannot tolerate architecture itself. Konrad Wachsmann, for example, tried to use industrialized and electronic exactitude to dissolve architecture, to design its exit in the name of an extreme hospitality. Wachsmann was an antiarchitect, deploying all the methods of the architectural discipline to undo that very discipline.[35]

Wachsmann's reputation is that of the preeminent expert in industrialized building systems, systematically mastering the practicalities of structure, fabrication, distribution, and organization. His original training as a cabinetmaker (before studying architecture and even working for a short time in the atelier of Le Corbusier and Pierre Jeanneret) was somehow visible in every project. He was famously obsessed with joints, the way things fit together, and produced a succession of ingenious, intricate, exquisite joints. The people who love Wachsmann, and there are many, seem to imagine that in a certain sense he holds the discipline together. To be, as it were, the caretaker of the idea of the joint is to be the caretaker of architecture, if architecture is thought of as the systematic assembly of parts into wholes. But the joints at the center of this image of practicality, tectonic rigor, systematization, and holding things together were actually the means of taking things apart. The Wachsmann project was to dismantle architecture. Wachsmann, almost always smoking and forever suspended in a cloud from his cigarette or cigar, wanted to dissolve buildings into an equally wispy cloud. Only as a cloud could architecture be genuinely hospitable, embracing diverse, mobile, changing, and unpredictable lives. Architecture as cloud, a kind of nonbuilding, would be open to the future, the always by definition surprising, even shocking, future. The idea of the architect making a stable object that stands against movement gave way to the idea of making a kind of moving ephemeral mirage.

Take Wachsmann's vast space frame hangar project for the US Air Force in 1950. It hangs there like a cloud in space without any of the elements of a traditional building—no floor, walls, roof, windows, or doors. But it could host those things if desired. More traditional architecture could be assembled within this frame, but the assembly would be temporary, a provisional performance rather than the illusion of a fixed object whose life extends beyond our own and is seen to house us by exceeding us. Here every gesture of fixing is a transitory statement. Even the frame hosting such statements is transitory and can be rapidly dismantled, reorganized, moved, or dissolved. A cloud is not just cloudy in the sense of blur but also in the sense that even the blur is always on the move and can disappear as quickly as it appeared.

This provisional cloud is precisely engineered. It is the very rigor of its single joint that allows all the forces to be distributed horizontally so it can float, and seem to be made of almost nothing. Precision parts are the basis of imprecise life, life even understood as imprecision. A remarkable joint that can receive up to twenty-one tubes at different angles at any point makes possible a woven porous fabric that acts as a kind of three-dimensional canvas for unlimited unpredictable statements. It touches the ground very lightly, like some huge insect, a flying insect perhaps. It is trying to be there as little as possible, even if this would be the biggest building on the planet—designed to house the aircraft with the biggest wingspan ever. It has no limit. The vast structure in Wachsmann's images is just a model of half an imagined typical installation that could theoretically be expanded infinitely.

It is an aircraft hangar, but maybe it is an aircraft, some alien craft that has just touched down or is about to take off. The human becomes a tiny figure, dwarfed by something astonishing, a sublime, bewildering phenomenon that could never simply be called an object. After all, there is no trace of the human in it, or else this is the strange unrecognized thing the human has become. Yet this absence of the human as traditionally understood might be precisely what it means to offer extreme hospitality to the human, to all possible future performances and understandings of the human.

Those into tectonics can only love the detail of the remarkable joint that makes this phenomenon possible. But Wachsmann insisted that at the heart of every joint—and this is emphasized in all his joints—is an emptiness. Structure, as it were, wraps itself around a hole. Architecture is made of holes. The perfect joint, the joint in which there is no difference between the joint and what it joins, allows for an ever finer distribution of holes. The perfect joint is the one that allows architecture to disappear. Wachsmann wanted to engineer that disappearance. Fixed forms had to give way to the endless flux of information.

Not by chance was Wachsmann's model Ruskin's nemesis, the Crystal Palace, not really a building but an industrialized system of distributing metal and glass that produced the effect of disappearing into a gauzy haze that was much commented on during the Great Exhibition. Likewise, the intricate weave of Wachsmann's hypnotically detailed models and drawings, their almost psychedelic layering of exactitude, aims to produce a haze in which architecture exits. This also means the exit of the figure of the architect as singular controlling agent. Wachsmann's own relationship to these projects is one of mystified bewilderment, just like the dwarfed human figures positioned below the models. Wachsmann pursues exactitude to its limit when exactitude finally becomes mystery.

Exactitude is, as it were, the medium in which architecture both appears and disappears. As such, it can never have the clarity that architecture aspires to. As the medium of architecture, it both excites and confuses architects. The intolerances of architecture, the architectural performance of exactitude, is the ultimately unsuccessful attempt to repress this. Or, to say it another way, exactitude is never exact.

NOTES

1 Le Corbusier, "L'Esprit Nouveau en architecture," lecture at Sorbonne, June 12, 1924, published in Le Corbusier, *Almanach d'architecture moderne* (Paris: G. Crès, 1925), 19.
2 Le Corbusier, *Vers une architecture* (Paris: G. Crès, 1923). The word "exactitude" is typically rendered in English translations as "precision" even if Le Corbusier uses all the variations of *précis* and *exacte* very specifically.
3 Ibid., 177.
4 Ibid., 192.
5 Ibid., 230.
6 Ibid., 240, 192.
7 Ibid., 231.
8 Le Corbusier, "L'Esprit Nouveau en architecture," 29.
9 Le Corbusier, *Urbanisme* (Paris: Editions G. Crès, 1924), ii.
10 Le Corbusier, "Un nouvel ordre de grandeur des éléments urbains, une

nouvelle unité d'habitation," *L'Ossature Metallique: Revue mensuelle des applications de l'acier* 3 no. 5 (May 1934): 239.

11 Le Corbusier and Willy Boesiger, eds., *Le Corbusier et Pierre Jeanneret oeuvre complete, 1910–1929* (Zurich: Editions Dr. H. Girsberger, 1943), 6.

12 Ibid., 5.

13 Le Corbusier, *Le Modulor, essai sur une mesure harmonique à l'échelle humaine, applicable universellement à l'architecture et à la mécanique* (1950), trans. Peter de Francia and Anna Bostock, in *The Modulor I & II* (Cambridge, MA: Harvard University Press, 1982), 136.

14 Le Corbusier, *Le Modulor II* (1955), in *The Modulor I & II*, 25, 297.

15 "That implacable exactitude expresses American taste. I see in it an effect of the machine." Le Corbusier, *When the Cathedrals Were White: A Journey to the Country of Timid People* (New York: Routledge, 1947), 159. "In America the rigor of exactitude is a pleasure. Idea of a masterpiece: exactitude." Ibid., 180.

16 *Vers une architecture*, 243, 241.

17 Ibid., 246.

18 Le Corbusier, "L'architecture et l'esprit mathématique" (1946), in *Le grands courants de la pensee mathematique: Presentes par F. Le Lionnais* (Paris: Cahiers du Sud, 1948), 490.

19 Le Corbusier, *Vers une architecture*, 174.

20 Antoine Babuty Desgodets, *Les édifices antiques de Rome dessinés et mesurés très exactement par Antoine Desgodetz, architecte* (Paris: Jean Baptiste Coignard, 1682).

21 "It is very important to reflect well on the exactitude of a judgement so precise that it would not be believable if experience did not bear it out." Claude Perrault, *Ordonnance des cinq especes de colonnes selon la methode des anciens* (1683), translated by Indra Kagis McEwen as *Ordonnance for the Five Kinds of Columns after the Method of the Ancients* (Los Angeles, CA: Getty Institute, 1993), 159.

22 "The exactitude of these proportions is not what makes the beauty of ancient buildings." Ibid, 59.

23 "Their proportions could not have the exactitude of the proportions that the first inventors of architecture gave them." Ibid., 68.

24 "In dimensioning of buildings, even today, as the workmen put together, a quarter inch is a perfectly good tolerance, but if you are building bearings for an automobile you can't have anything like that. So the automobile men get down to ten thousands of an inch. In building airplanes today and the space rocketry, where mild variations and enormous velocities are going to build-in errors, they are dealing in a millionth of an inch. But the building world is still a quarter of an inch kind of stuff. I couldn't have any such nonsense as that when I really was going to get into the geodesics, so really I was out to see how I really could reduce stress in forces. . . . We kept the tolerance to lo,oooths of an inch! Now bringing a lo,oooth of an inch into a big building where the quarter of an inch had been fine, you can imagine the general contractors when I faced them, they said you can't have any nonsense like this, so I said 'I have designed all of the tooling, I have designed all of your logistics, as general contractors, simply, I will handle the whole thing for you.'" Buckminster

Fuller, "Everything I Know," Session 8, 1975, transcript by Buckminster Fuller Institute.

25 The machine is "shaped with a theoretical precision and exactitude *which can never be seen in nature itself.*" Le Corbusier, *L'Art décoratif d'aujourd'hui* (1925), translated by James Dummet as *The Decorative Art of Today* (Cambridge, MA: MIT Press, 1987), 112.

26 Ibid., 95.

27 Leon Battista Alberti, *De re aedificatoria*, book 6, chap. 10.

28 Ibid., book 6, chap. 5.

29 Ibid., book 9, chap. 9.

30 John Ruskin, *The Opening of the Crystal Palace Considered in Some of Its Relations to the Prospects of Art* (London: Smith, Elder, 1854), 8.

31 John Ruskin, letter to his father, dated October 1, 1845. Harold Shapiro, *Ruskin in Italy, Letters to His Parents, 1845* (London: Clarendon Press, 1972), 218.

32 John Ruskin letter to his father, dated October 7, 1845. Ibid., 220.

33 John Ruskin, "The Relation to Art of the Sciences of Organic Form," in *The Eagle's Nest: Ten Lectures on the Relation of Natural Science to Art, Given before the University of Oxford, 1872* (London: George Allen, 1900), 137.

34 John Ruskin, "The Power of Contentment in Science and Art," in *The Eagle's Nest*, 83.

35 See Mark Wigley, *Konrad Wachsmann's Television: Post-Architectural Transmissions* (Berlin: Sternberg Press, 2020).

Chapter 2

New Narratives in the After-Post-Truth Age

Posthumanism, Precision, and Conservation

Alejandro Zaera-Polo

> Postmodernism, the school of "thought" that proclaimed "There are no truths, only interpretations[,]" has largely played itself out in absurdity, but it has left behind a generation of academics in the humanities disabled by their distrust of the very idea of truth and their disrespect for evidence, settling for "conversations" in which nobody is wrong and nothing can be confirmed, only asserted with whatever style you can muster.
> —Daniel C. Dennett on *Wieseltier v. Pinker* in *The New Republic*

Beyond becoming a global catastrophe and a huge disturbance for all of us, COVID-19 signals the dawn of an era. While the combined effects of the September 11, 2001 attacks, and the 2007 global financial crisis had already damaged the integrity of so-called neoliberalism beyond repair, COVID-19, the most brutal face of climate change and environmental degradation, marks the beginning of an entirely different regime that will require a different mindset.

COVID-19 has confirmed the radical effects of nonhuman populations—in this case, viruses—on the design and performance

FIGURE 2.1. Ruins of the Enlightenment Project, waiting for the COVID-19 resurrection. Institute of Legal Medicine, Madrid, Spain, 2008 AZPML Ltd.

of cities, and the overwhelming relevance of scientific determinations to the fields of architecture and urbanism. Social distancing, confinement, the physics of airborne volatile organic compounds and other ruthless biopolitics suggest what we had long suspected: that architectural and urban "cultures" are an irrelevant efflorescence of the true forces of urban and architectural evolution.

The post-truth era and its political consequences, populism and identity politics, may have been the death rattle of postmodernism. The emerging conflict between ecological imperatives and social justice, as illustrated by the *gilets jaunes*[1] struggle against environmental taxes to defend the all-important right to drive a car with an internal combustion engine, is a vivid example of these confrontations.

In the face of the futile attempts at a disciplinary revival from some contemporary architects, primarily driven by Byzantine discussions about style and language, and the demagogic pretense of social constructivists and other politically correct, human-driven activisms in architecture (of class, gender, race, etc.) that we have seen flourish in recent years, COVID-19 has suddenly returned us to more fundamental issues: the most relevant concerns for the design of buildings and cities, now and in the near future, are related not to humans but to nonhuman processes and populations, such as carbon emissions, environmental pollution, pervasive computation, artificial sensing, and the concentration of volatile organic components.

As a result, a return to technical expertise, exactitude, and scientific evidence as the very basis of our practice may eventually put an end to the staggering dilettantism that the disciplinary discourse in architecture has promoted for four decades. Exactitude may become the alternative to the relentless drive toward the artificial construction of difference that has engulfed speculative architectural practices. In construction parlance, COVID-19 may lead us into a new range of intolerances in our practices and discourses.

If postmodernism promoted an immaterial architecture based on authorship, the new intolerances will revolve around the physical and the concrete. Social distances, megajoules per kilogram of embodied energy, thermal transmittances, emitted carbon dioxide per kilogram, construction weight per square meter, concentrations of particulate matter 2.5, and volatile organic components have turned postmodern authorship into a vacuous ambition.

The postmodern compulsion to produce original, different interpretations of the world appears to be ineffective to address the biopolitics of COVID-19 and the undeniable evidence of global warming. The intensification of difference and the mobilization of affects are no longer an effective approach to the city of the near future. Affects appear as a shortsighted endeavor in the Anthropocene, when architecture needs to address problems that transcend human sensibilities. The exponential rise of an artificial environmental sensibility suggests that the very notion of the human subject has to be revised and connected to environmental processes, as Jennifer Gabrys has so brilliantly described.[2]

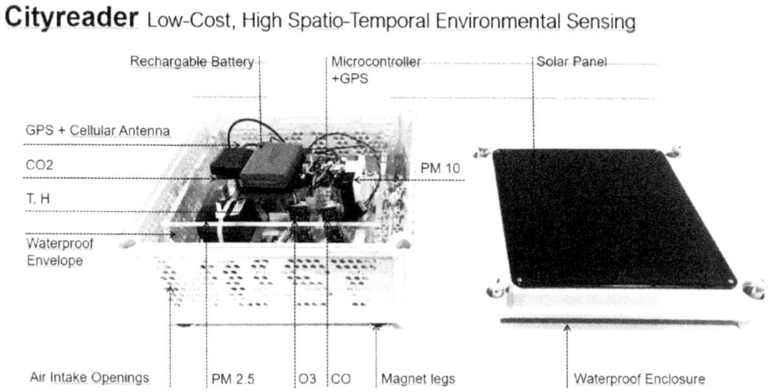

Cityreader Low-Cost, High Spatio-Temporal Environmental Sensing

Rechargable Battery | Microcontroller +GPS | Solar Panel

GPS + Cellular Antenna
CO2
T, H
Waterproof Envelope

PM 10

Air Intake Openings | PM 2.5 | O3 | CO | Magnet legs | Waterproof Enclosure

FIGURE 2.2. Program Earth, sensing kit for high spatio-temporal resolution environmental sensing. AZPML Ltd. 2017.

COVID-19 signals the end of manners: postmodern representation and scenography will be soon replaced by ruthless choreographies of proxemic distance and biometric recognition, where measurability and quantification—the *matters of fact* rather than the *matters of concern*—become crucial, and where the naked eye is insufficient. It is the minute detail of the face, rather than the obvious gestures and representations, that matters. Measurement and quantification are the most powerful antidote against the post-truth, against populism and identity politics, by introducing new sensibilities of alienation in the Brechtian sense.

The "Difference Engine" versus Posthuman Alienation

We are genetically 99.5% alike. But we spend 99.5% of our time focused on that 0.5% that is different.
—Bill Clinton at the Omega Institute's Center for Sustainable Living, October 5, 2013

The Democrats—the longer they talk about identity politics, I got them. I want them to talk about racism every day. If the left is focused on race and identity, and we go with economic nationalism, we can crush the Democrats.
—Steve Bannon, in an interview with Robert Kuttner, in *The American Prospect*, August 16, 2017

The two quotes given above vividly illustrate the current political dilemma. Clinton's reference to the Human Genome Project offers a posthuman perspective on the question of difference, while Bannon's project is constructed on the intensification of difference through race and nationalism.[3] Postmodern culture was grounded in expanding tolerances for the sake of promoting democracy but has now become an engine to produce difference for its own sake. And while tolerance for different opinions is a trait of a democratic culture, it may be that it is also at the origin of the post-truth world, as Lee McIntyre argues in his book *Post-Truth*.[4] As in the quote from Daniel C. Dennett that opens this chapter, all the polite relativism, those "interpretations" and "conversations," have produced an endemic "mistrust of truth and evidence where anything goes and nothing is right or wrong, and everything can be stated in whatever style you can muster."[5] Kellyanne Conway's reference to "alternative facts" is often cited as one of the paradigmatic examples of the post-truth, progressively splitting reality into multiple, parallel, and disconnected universes. Not even evolutionary theory or climate change are considered any longer proven, let alone, say, architecture's environmental performance.

And yet, architecture's environmental performance seems to be not just a worthwhile common ground and endeavor but also a model where multiple entities are necessarily bound with each other into a system that transcends them as classes, types and identities. Is political ecology the alternative to the politics of identity and populism? Should we suspend human concerns to be able to retrieve a common thread between these diverging universes? Can the natural sciences become our lingua franca?

Furthermore, social media has made cultural values more quantifiable than ever. We have now access to technologies increasingly capable of capturing—and manipulating—collective values and opinions. The idea that culture is irreducible to quantification is entirely misguided and reactionary: cultural identity can no longer be used as an excuse for exceptionalism. Amazon knows what we are going to buy tomorrow through their microtargeting algorithms, psychographs, and data mining. Social and cultural behavior is increasingly predictable. This is not exclusive to Western cultures. Steve Bannon and Dominic Cummings can predict how we are going to vote with an amazing degree of precision.

If social and cultural behavior is now measurable, we should be able to transcend cultural, religious, racial, and gender divides. And yet, the percentage of Black academics working on blackness, female academics working on feminist critique, and non-Western academics working on postcolonialism and the Global South is overwhelming. As if knowledge were inevitably circumscribed by contingent biological and cultural determinations, academic administrators are increasingly driven to the artificial creation of difference. The controversy around the translation of Amanda Gorman's verses into Dutch and Catalonian early in 2021 is an example of what the intensification of difference around identities has led us to.[6] Isn't the very purpose of knowledge and science to free us from these biological, territorial, and cultural determinations?

I believe that, unlike those identity-based practices, alienation, estrangement (*Verfremdung* in Brecht's parlance), gender-bending, and other forms of the erasure of identity have a much higher liberating potential. The contemporary politics of identity condemns the practice of architecture—and the discipline—to a hopelessly provincial fragmentation and the perpetual representation of clichés and stereotypes—of gender, race, origin, belief, culture, and so forth. This closes possibilities for architecture to construct new worlds instead of merely representing them.

Rather than the politics of identity, I favor the politics of becoming, which challenges the hard segmentations between identities that populisms are trying to force upon us. Like Jessica Krug, the professor who pretended to be Black; like Paul Preciado (formerly known as Beatriz Preciado) changing their gender through "molecular" testosterone injections, like Rudyard Kipling becoming Hindi, becoming a Pariah. . . . there is a long history of creolization and hybridization that I believe to be truly productive culturally: it is precisely the possibility to operate outside defined identities that has come under attack of populisms and identity politics, the extrapolations of cultural difference. In the face of the deluge of relativism, and its post-truth derivations populism and identity-based politics, it may be worth looking at some imperial, low-threshold protocols aimed at producing consistency across geographically and culturally diverse populations and their capacity to free their subjects from tribal forms of power based on land, ethnicity, cultural tradition, or religion by reducing laws to their minimum common denominator.[7]

Both populisms and identity politics promote a craft based on representation and "molar" perceptions. Instead, I am interested on the politics of becoming and the architecture that derives from them, which is one based on material intensities, as in Gilles Deleuze and Félix Guattari's "becoming-intense, becoming-animal, becoming imperceptible."[8] I am for an architecture that eschews the clichés of representation and language and their drastic reductions of reality, to engage directly with the material world and its intensities, looking at matter on a molecular imperceptible level. Scientific exactitude and quantitative analysis also imply the development of a different scale of perception and sensibility: close attention to detail and an alienating perception have now acquired a much higher liberating potential than the politics of identity.

Against the obvious gesticulations and human-driven poles of populisms and identity politics, we can mobilize an exact, intolerant architecture that looks at the imperceptible, the chemical, and the molecular—the turbulent eddies in a flow instead of its laminar behavior, the molecular reactions in a chemical compound or the ultralow perceptual thresholds that allow a facial recognition algorithm to recognize identity, individual identity for the masses that crave recognition. The skeptics will state that scientific analysis and data may be manipulated or wrong, but I am prepared to take the risk: it is lower than the risks of the post-truth. Ultimately, Charles Babbage's words strongly resonate for me when he states that "Errors using inadequate data are much less than those using no data at all."[9]

One of my favorite stories about the role of architecture in identity politics took place at the Berlage Institute circa 1990, over a decade before 9/11, when the cracks of the neoliberal system started to appear with respect to the violent eruption of Islamic fundamentalism, one of the most aggressive forms of identity politics.[10] The Portuguese architect Alvaro Siza had just completed a residential project in the Schilderswijk Ward in The Hague. The Dutch architect Herman Hertzberger invited Siza to present the project at the Berlage

Institute. Both Siza and Hertzberger are self-proclaimed progressives: Siza is a veteran of the Revoluçao dos Claveles, and Hertzberger is the paladin of the Dutch welfare state. Siza presented his project and explained that he had been told that most of the tenants were from a North African background and were strict Muslim believers. The project revolved around a reinterpretation of the traditions of Dutch residential projects, like brick walls and walk-up stairs, but he also designed a sliding door that allowed the units to split the living room into a public and a private zone where women could retreat, preserving the traditional etiquette of Muslim inhabitants.

After Siza's presentation, Hertzberger praised the project but said that public housing in the Netherlands should not support social habits that ran counter to Dutch morality and its belief in gender equality. Was the exfoliation of the private/public threshold to the interior of the unit a politically advanced decision, appropriate for a tolerant, multicultural society? Or was it a sign of unacceptable political behavior that defied the most basic definitions of universal human rights and democracy? While Hertzberger was, politically speaking, right, Siza's project was a demonstration of how material complexities can sometimes articulate social complexities that cannot be resolved through identity politics. Hertzberger represented an unflinchingly raw political perspective, while Siza engaged in an opportunistic spatial process that refused to be entirely captured into identity politics, fractious or universal. This event predates by almost fifteen years the assault on multicultural Britain by Trevor Phillips, then chairman of the Commission for Racial Equality in the United Kingdom, in his famous interview in the *Times* on April 3, 2004, and Jacques Chirac's French law on secularism and conspicuous religious symbols in schools (also known as *laïcité*) that came into effect on September 2, 2004. I believe that both Chirac and Phillips were attacking an emerging identity-driven violence, just like Hertzberger a decade before. But I wonder if Siza's approach would not have been more effective at resolving the conflicts that would eventually trigger 9/11. Concerning architecture, matter and geometry prove to be more ductile than identity politics: that is why identity politics always produces such stiff architecture![11]

The currency of architecture as a key discipline capable of putting an end to the post-truth lies in the fact that it is fundamentally driven by physical and environmental concerns. Building physics work across cultures: a radiator or a sunshade works with the same principles everywhere: each just reacts differently to the local climates. Of course, there are differences, just like there are differences in the behavior of a chiller between the American Northeast and Southern China. You cannot have the same type of democracy in China and in America. But still, there is a political regime called democracy in which people can participate to different degrees in the regimes of power. And there are carbon emission ratios and thermal transmittance or ventilation values that apply equally to genders and races. And I believe it is important to defend these values as universal.

In fact, architects are optimally positioned to drive the necessary reduction of tolerances to escape from the post-truth. Some undeniable truths in architecture defy social constructivism. For example, gravity cannot, I am afraid, be socially constructed, although one may fake weightlessness. But no matter how light one wants to make one's building look, it will have a weight, as Fuller famously stated. And an architect ought to know it. I would go even further in suggesting that one also needs to know the envelope ratio, the fenestration ratio, the average U-value, the average energy consumption per square meter, and the embodied energy and carbon emissions per square meter of our buildings. And one needs to keep them under certain tolerances.

We may have to go back to these arcane questions of architecture, which are becoming increasingly measurable and intelligible. We may also need to produce a set of values that we can demonstrate to the wider public, so that we can change the public sensibility away from theatrical gestures, which are predominant under both the neoliberal regimes and in their populist and identity-based nemesis. The time has come for a new set of intolerances in architecture: buildings with inadequate facade ratios, materials with high-embodied energy or inefficient performance, complex structures that increase their steel weight, and sealed buildings that require forced ventilation or air-based environmental conditioning may have to be excluded from the relevant practices by a new wave of intolerance.

FIGURE 2.3. A new authenticity, Fundación Cerezales, Leon, Spain, 2017, AZPML Ltd.

New Authenticity, Radical Measurability, and "Neocon" Architecture?

COVID-19 signals the return of "truth" and expertise after the catastrophic failures of relativism and interpretation, and their blatant resonance with the mistrust of facts and evidence that fuels the ideologies of climate change deniers, intelligent design promoters, "patriots," and other post-truth thugs. The extravagance, the widespread exceptionalism of the last few decades of architecture—the city of exceptions—has consolidated architecture as one of the postmodern practices. And yet, architecture is a hyperconcrete, quantifiable practice in terms of its most crucial performances. In the face of increasing cultural fragmentation, I believe that architecture is ideally situated to promote the idea of a "single truth" that we can approximate through quantification—be it weight, daylight levels, insulation, carbon emissions, or embodied energy—rather than being focused on the creation of "alternative truths" and the theater of difference.

A new authenticity is certainly a central claim of populisms: after the artificiality of the neoliberal world, some architects are already successfully exploring this by seeking alignments with local imagery, cultural precedents, and other identity traits. Activism, multiculturalism, and diversity have developed their own forms of architectural representation to replace the floating signifier of the neoliberal star architect: architecture connects to local communities and represents "the people" rather than global capital. Alejandro Aravena, Liu Jiakun, Wang Shu, and other apostles of authenticity in architecture preach a critique of neoliberal architectural extravagance and a return to community or to construction as the reservoirs of architectural truthfulness. Theirs is a human-driven truth, based on community and identity.

Alternatively, a radical return to measurability and quantification is also emerging as an alternative ground for authenticity. From Forensis and Carlo Ratti to Kieran Timberlake and our own practice, a growing number of architects eschew representation in favor of technically augmented measurability: geolocation, sensors, and point clouds are newly available tools to form architectural essences in the after-post-truth. These practices are more invested in exploring the artificial sensibilities of point clouds, facial recognition, thermal imagery, and machine learning instead of focusing on representation and interpretation. A radical return to a single truth, to measurability and quantification, in the most arcane, truth-seeking, modernist key, is our favored alternative to develop an after-post-truth sensibility.

Of course, this position carries risks: the postmodernists and the relativists will immediately say that science is always biased and cannot be trusted. That is exactly the argument systematically leveled by the proponents of alternative facts, climate change deniers, intelligent design supporters, and all those invested in exploiting doubt and "interpretation." to manufacture truth through powerful computational tools: truth is multiple, truth is cultural, truth is human.[12] And yet, these posthuman politicians such as Steve Bannon, Robert Mercer, and Dominic Cummings are using bots and big data mining to build their constituencies. The new precisions of geolocation, artificial sensing, big data, and machine learning outline the production of new forms of evidence that may reduce substantially the need for interpretation, which may be used as a legitimation of authority: Friedrich Nietzsche wrote (perhaps forecasting the post-truth world that in a world where everything is an interpretation), "Truth is merely a function of power."[13] Massive amounts of "good enough data" can aggregate to produce intelligence that does not rely on a human perspective, in which we may discover new and unexpected architectural truths to inaugurate the posthuman sensibilities of the after-post-truth.[14]

The question is, then, how do we ground the new architectural "truths"? Unlike social media, architecture's retreat into representation and identity politics is not entirely possible. The fakeness of architecture can only be partially achieved, as it is—at least in its customary form—inevitably bound to the physical construction of the real. We have all seen the affects of the PoMo architecture and its deconstructivist and stellar derivations and their fake materiality. If there is something that architecture can do to confront the post-truth world, it is to abandon postmodern relativism and alternative facts and commit to a single truth, much like in the most rancid modern manifestos about constructive sincerity, happy bricks, béton brut, structural transparency, and the elimination of poché. . . . It is precisely the lack of material corporeality that makes it possible to turn architecture into a pure representation. Dematerialization is a precondition of representation, identity politics, and social constructivism, and, perhaps, even relativism. After all, the physical principles of building cannot be socially constructed, and are particularly important in the era of global warming, environmental degradation and COVID-19. This involves a radical return to matter, including the chemical, molecular scale of chromosomes, DNA chains, and testosterone and estrogen levels . . . which places a limit on the human—and humanist—construction of reality. Is this return to matter, to chemistry, a hopelessly conservative position or a necessary posthuman expansion that is in fact progressive and inclusive, as in the example of the Siza dwellings in Schilderswijk?

Disembodiment is, paradoxically, the precondition for representation, the politics of identity and social constructivism, and, perhaps, even relativism. But after all, building physics cannot be socially constructed. If the optimization of matter and space became redundant in the 1970s, when building technologies were driven by unlimited access to energy and cheap matter, suddenly it is important to go back to the precise calibration of the material and energy consumption we use to build and maintain buildings and cities, and to consider the interference with the natural cycles of water, carbon, nitrogen, biodiversity . . . Precise calculation and optimization of transformation processes material make sense once again.

If the neoliberal world order associated the progressive with the novel, with the extravagant and the excessive, we are now in an age in which the exhaustion of natural resources, pollution, and global warming have become a universal concern, and in which excess is unwarranted. Urban metabolism needs to be reduced to a minimum. Conservation—of energy, of biodiversity, of the urban fabric, of the environment—has become a growing concern that far exceeds the "conservation of cultural values," which architects embraced some time ago and is now generally accepted by the public.

Progressive narratives appear to be aligning now with a conservative approach. Scores of architects are moving away from formal experimentation and seeking refuge in traditional architectural models, typologies, geometries, tectonics, and conventions. In the political arena, the emergence of a culturally driven, anticommercial, and politically correct neo-avant-garde has proposed a return to either disciplinary autonomy or political engagement in the traditional sense as a form of resistance to neoliberal exuberance and excess. *San Rocco Magazine* is probably one of the best examples of this contemporary trend toward convention, indifference, eclecticism, historicism, and high culture. In the mainstream media, populist critics such as Oliver Wainwright and Michael Kimmelman, who advocate an exit from the neoliberal excess through politically correct architecture that is modest, socially constructed, and physically conservative.

Conservation has come to replace novelty: instead of radical transformation and tabula rasa, contemporary architectural values are retreating toward convention, continuity, and history. Is it possible to escape the regression of a "cultured," historiographical neo-avant-garde? Is it possible to escape from cultural and historical preservation, representing identities, community building, and even tectonics and phenomenology as the only alternative to the "city of exceptions" and the neoliberal, populist appetite for novelty?

This neoconservativism of late, and particularly its postmodern avant-garde versions—populist or elitist—demand a critique capable of discerning its historical dimensions. The distinction is particularly

FIGURE 2.4. Urban recycling, Palacinema Locarno, Locarno, Switzerland, 2017
AZPML Ltd.

relevant at a time when populisms on the left and the right are reclaiming ideology as a necessary component of practice. When does the conservative shift from an evolutionary to a devolutionary approach? How can we define in architectural terms the equivalents of consuetudinary law, adaptation, evolution, and perhaps even "true-blue" and Republican values? Whether we subscribe to these or not, the organic, evolutionary nature of right-wing traditional politics is certainly a precedent to consider if architecture needs to aim for slowness and conservation rather than quick transformation through ideology. It is a fine line to walk before a public audience that has now become accustomed to strident gestures and artistic manners, and has lost its sensibility for nuances—or that is retreating into a conservative architecture after suffering from vertigo. Is a progressive conservationism at all possible?

Modern architects attempted to emancipate themselves from the powerful and work for "the people." But their devices were primarily representational and linguistic: "the people" could perceive progressive architecture as a language with democratizing affects such as long windows, liberating *pilotis,* or wholesome *cities in the garden.* Modern architecture was enthralled by these linguistic games. Postmodernist critics decided then that the discipline was about playing with those elements, voiding them from their original performances. The discipline became self-referential and lost the virtuous cachet of modernism. Fast-forwarding history, we get to deconstructivism and its disruption of modernist tropes. The discipline revolved around disrupting authority through representation and became entirely self-referential: architects kept twisting things to defy gravity, the definitive symbol of authority and stability. Gravity, symmetry, and order became symbols of power to be defied by the discipline, which was operating on a purely representational dimension.

In some of the recent architectural critique, we can find the resurgence of this idea of the disciplinary, as a form of resistance against the submission to the neoliberal order and the associated end of history. Unfortunately, this is just a theatrical, fake resistance, because the real power play occurs outside these disciplinary games now.

Retrieving some of the traits of "conservative" architecture—such as symmetry, compactness, gravity, regularity, and order—detached from their symbolic associations may be a relevant endeavor for the after-post-truth. By the end of World War II, there were few, if any, advocates of symmetry left. Scholars such as Rudolph Arnheim, Ernst Gombrich, and Bruno Zevi had co-opted symmetry as the visible face of fascism, an order that is imposed onto an "organic" reality characterized fundamentally by "creative" asymmetry. Symmetry became banal, boring, and static, embodying a primitive form of order that offered a limited view of reality. Zevi routinely decried it as a blunt representation of authoritarianism. And yet, symmetrical organizations have extraordinary properties when analyzed from a performative—rather than representational—perspective. In fact, they tend to outperform asymmetrical organizations on many functions. Isn't it time to look at these spatial, material, and organizational traits from a performative viewpoint, and to develop their agencies?

An architecture of exactness and quantification that operates "under the radar"—sometimes even on a chemical level—may be more effective to connect the building to wider material ecologies. It may also form an alternative to tectonic and phenomenological gestures and manifest identities. COVID-19, as an index of environmental degradation and climate change, and our much-expanded capacity to measure and simulate will drive us toward

FIGURE 2.5. Twisted symmetry, Austro Tower Vienna, under construction, 2021, AZPML Ltd.

building-physics conservativism rather than extravagant, "socially constructed" tectonics. A neocon architecture will do away with instability, fragmentation, difference, dynamism, asymmetry, and other postmodern tropes. Can we possibly reclaim symmetry, hierarchy, order, regularity, compactness, stability, and repetition as progressive architectural traits in defiance of established contemporary wisdom? Since modernism, some of these material and geometrical traits have become the indexes of conservatism and authoritarian politics—as in Zevi's association between symmetry and fascism. This reading may be entirely reversed when contemplated from a performative (not representational) perspective. In fact, many of these traits are more likely to produce buildings with better environmental performance, programmatic flexibility, and an economy of resources.

My hypothesis for our practice is that we need to embrace these new intolerances and eschew the representational drive of the discipline. We may have to design compact and symmetrical buildings to reduce envelope ratios and adaptability; we may need to use light and prefabricated construction to reduce embodied energy and construction waste, or timber to capture carbon. We find this self-restraint increasingly exciting.

FIGURE 2.6. Material recycling, Korean Museum of Architecture and Urbanism, Sejong City, Korea, 2020, AZPML Ltd.

NOTES

1 The *gilets jaunes* is a populist, grassroots protest movement for economic justice that began in France in October 2018. The protesters called for lower fuel taxes, wealth taxation, an increased minimum wage, and the implementation of citizens' initiative referendums. Yellow high-visibility vests, which French law requires all drivers to have in their vehicles to wear during emergencies, were chosen as "a unifying thread and call to arms" because of their convenience, visibility, ubiquity, and association with working-class industries. "Yellow Vests Protests," Wikipedia, https://en.wikipedia.org/wiki/Yellow_vests_movement, accessed September 17, 2021.

2 Jennifer Gabrys, *Program Earth: Environmental Sensing Technology and the Making of a Computational Planet* (Minneapolis: University of Minnesota Press), 2016.

3 Honeybee Capital Foundation, "What President Clinton Taught Me about Empathy This Weekend," https://www.honeybeecapital.org/20131006/what-president-clinton-taught-me-about-empathy-this-weekend/, accessed September 17, 2021.

4 See Lee C. McIntyre, *Post-Truth* (Cambridge, MA: MIT Press, 2018), 123–50.

5 Daniel C. Dennett, "Dennett on Wieseltier V. Pinker in The New Republic: Let's Start with a Respect for Truth," Edge.org, September 9, 2013, https://www.edge.org/conversation/daniel_c_dennett-dennett-on-wieseltier-v-pinker-in-the-new-republic.

6 See Alison Flood, "'Shocked by the Uproar': Amanda Gorman's White Translator Quits," https://wwwtheguardian.com/books/2021/mar/01/amanda-gorman-white-translator-quits-marieke-lucas-rijneveld, accessed September 17, 2021; and AFP Barcelona, "'Not Suitable': Catalan Translator for Amanda Gorman Poem Removed," https://www.theguardian.com/books/2021/mar/10/not-suitable-catalan-translator-for-amanda-gorman-poem-removed, accessed September 17, 2021.

7 In *The Places in Between* (Orlando: Harcourt, 2006), Rory Stewart—former UK conservative MP fired by the populist politician Boris Johnson, spy, explorer, walker, and now Yale academic—describes the efforts by the British colonial rulers to understand their subjects (unlike contemporary fundamentalists, who believe that Western democracy can be universally imposed).

8 See "1730: Becoming-Intense, Becoming-Animal, Becoming-Imperceptible," *A Thousand Plateaus: Capitalism and Schizophrenia*, by Gilles Deleuze and Félix Guattari, 232–309.

9 "Of Price as Measured by Money," in *On the Economy of Machinery and Manufactures*, by Charles Babbage (London: Charles Knight, Pall Mall East, 1836), 156.

10 "The Politics of the Envelope," in *The Sniper's Log: Architectural Chronicles of Generation X*, by Alejandro Zaera-Polo (Barcelona: Actar, 2012), 530–31.

11 Xi Jinping's "No more weird architecture" or Donald Trump's "Executive Order on Promoting Beautiful Federal Civic Architecture from Dec. 21st, 2020" are interesting examples on a high level of sclerotic architecture. But there are multiple examples of the physical rawness of "activist" architecture.

12 "Doubt is our product since it is the best means of competing with the 'body of fact' that exists in the minds of the general public." From an infamous 1969 memo sent by an executive at Brown & Williamson tobacco, a subsidiary of R. J. Reynolds Tobacco Company.

13 Friedrich Nietzsche, *Daybreak: Thoughts on the Prejudices of Morality* (Cambridge: Cambridge University Press, 1995), 39.

14 Jennifer Gabrys, Helen Pritchard, and Benjamin Barratt, "Just Good Enough Data: Figuring Data Citizenships through Air Pollution Sensing and Data Stories," *Big Data & Society* 3, no. 2 (2016): https://journals.sagepub.com/doi/full/10.1177/2053951716679677, accessed September 17, 2021.

Chapter 3

Verify in Field

Verification and Materiality in Contemporary
Design Workflow

Eric Höweler

Verify in Field, or VIF, is a notational convention employed
on architectural drawings indicating that the information on the drawings is incomplete, and further field measurement
and verification are necessary. The term reveals the gap between
design intent and built reality. It also acknowledges our collective
disciplinary investments in the instruments of design—the drawings, models, and prototypes that are the discipline's means for
operating on the world *at a distance.*

"Verification," in this case, may refer to a field dimension, alignment, or survey point. It may also refer to a process of feedback,
where information and expertise are fed back into the design process in ways that inflect the original design. Or, as I hope to show in
this essay, "verification" may include factors involving the political
and environmental contexts for design.

The "field," as construction site, is understood to be outside the
scope of the architect. It is the space of contingencies, externalities,
and uncertainties. While VIF can be understood as a disclaimer,

architecture's "fine print," as it were, the notation speaks volumes about the discipline and the profession: our culture of risk, the role of representation, and our agency to act on the physical world.

Verify in Field cleaves apart conception from construction, model from building, representation from execution, and architect from builder. Beyond a strict delineation of scope, risk, and responsibility, the separation of representation from building is significant for how we conceptualize disciplinary practices, especially as these evolve with new technologies and digital design practices.

As Robin Evans and others have argued, drawings precede buildings, and are thus the primary site of the architect's art.[1] The completed building was understood as the "objective" of the drawing. Yet contemporary drawings are not drawings at all but vector information, often assembled as digital models, blocks, and data. Contemporary design workflows are altering the assumed sequences of priority and precedence, introducing new instrumentality to drawings and models as fabrication tools and challenging the inherited hierarchy between buildings and models. At the same time, the status of the physical building as well as its materials are being reassessed. Post occupancy evaluations, life-cycle analyses, and material obsolescence also question the notion of the building as the *end* point of design: the completed building often *initiates* another series of models that have to do with monitoring user behavior and energy consumption. While Verify in Field, at its most mundane level, addresses the physical and contingent conditions of construction, I understand this term as an operating principle to frame contemporary design processes and develop the means for more agency, responsibility, and engagement.

To give an example, a shop drawing shows the interface between the precast panel and window wall system. The dotted lines represent a combination of facade erection tolerance, precast fabrication tolerance, and precast erection tolerance. Not shown in this diagram are deflection tolerances, concrete creep, column shortening, and live load deflections. When all these factors are combined, the joint could be either 1¼ inch or ⅜ inch wide. The "acceptable range" of joint width varies by ⅝ inch and is absorbed by the compressible backer rod and caulk. The multiple possible acceptable geometries of fabrication and erection point to the *unknowability* of the actual conditions in the field, and the necessity of techniques for tolerance.

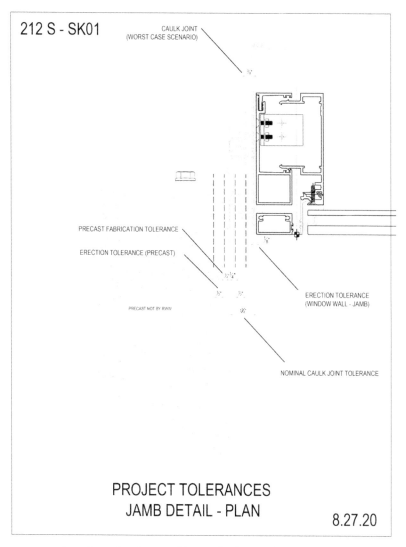

FIGURE 3.1. Stuart Street shop drawing of the interface between the precast concrete panel and aluminum window wall frame, with the different tolerances highlighted in the joint width. Courtesy of Höweler + Yoon.

In this essay, I will elaborate on three projects by Höweler + Yoon through the lens of "verification" and "field" conditions. In each case, the project involved questions of fabrication and precision, erection, and tolerance, and necessitated continuous feedback loops between model and material, shop, and field. The three projects also defined "field" in different ways: the "field of construction," the "field of public engagement," and finally the "field of environmental thinking."

The Sean Collier Memorial was built in response to the killing of MIT public safety officer Sean Collier, who was shot by the Tsarnaev brothers after the Boston Marathon bombing on April 18, 2013. In the following days, an informal memorial sprang up on MIT's campus as people sought a form of expression for their grief. In response to the marathon bombings, a campaign emerged to remain *strong*: "Boston Strong," "MIT Strong," and "Collier Strong." Strength, it seemed, was the response to domestic terror. We asked ourselves if strength and structure might offer clues about the appropriate response to the memorial design.

Our design concept was to create a figure that could convey a sense of "conspicuous absence." We chose to carve a boulder-like figure out of a five-fingered form. We wanted the visitors to come face to face with a missing figure whose contours were inscribed at the intersection of the void and the walls. Additionally, we proposed to make the figure into an arch, or vault, constructed of solid stone blocks. The principle of the arch is that all blocks transfer loads to adjacent blocks until they meet the ground.

The challenge of building an arch with today's construction techniques introduced some complexity. True compression arches ceased to be built when steel-reinforced concrete and veneer masonry replaced arches at the beginning of the twentieth century. Discussions between our engineers and the contractor worked through questions of sequence and constructability. Computer modeling by our structural engineers and masonry consultants resulted in different solutions based on different assumptions. They did, however, agree that the shallowness of the arch meant that the structure was very "deflection sensitive," and the stone blocks would need to fit together with a high degree of precision. Small horizontal displacements would mean significant vertical displacements.

The various models employed in the conception and construction of the Sean Collier Memorial exemplify contemporary digital workflows relative to modeling, simulation, and verification. The procurement of stone required blocks larger than the industry standard blocks that are optimized for slabbing for kitchen counters. Searching for blocks suitable for the keystone required special procurement at the quarry, and several rounds of adjustments to the block geometry to fit within the bounding box of the quarriable and transportable stone blocks. We field verified all the blocks to ensure that the expected block geometries would fit within the dimensions of the rough-cut quarry blocks.

We also began discussions about fabrication equipment, capabilities, and tolerances. The fabrication process involved translating the geometrical model that we produced into a fabrication model to be used by the fabricator to carve the finished blocks. This involved a series of different tools, including CNC saws and multi-axis industrial robots. The use of our 3D model for fabrication introduced questions of responsibility, liability, and quality control. During a traditional process, the architect's drawings are for design intent only. The fabricator typically produces their own shop drawings for fabrication, and the shop drawing review process allows for quality control.

Since we considered the architect's 3D model files as "deliverables," they essentially became fabrication files, thus requiring rethinking the processes of quality assurance and quality control. Shop tickets for specific blocks were fabricated based on digital files, but then each block was subsequently dimensionally checked in the shop before shipping.

As members of the architectural profession, we tend to have great confidence in digital tools. Francesca Hughes refers to this overconfidence as a fetish of precision, which creates unrealistic expectations of material, and relegates exceptions to the category of "error."[2] In fabricating the Sean Collier Memorial, we came to understand the limits of precision as they related to material processes. With every pass of the digital saw, the stone block was carved away, approaching the final geometry of the designed block. We had a set of x-, y-, and z-coordinates that told us the precise dimensions of the stone and where the stone was supposed

FIGURE 3.2. Fabrication of stone blocks for the Sean Collier Memorial involves a multi-axis robot with a large work envelope. Courtesy of Höweler + Yoon.

to begin and end. Yet during the fabrication process, Jim Durham, the fabricator, and owner of Quarra Stone, asked us, "Where is the interface between the saw blade and the stone?" and "How do you know that the stone is precise if the saw is also wearing down with each pass?" This question about the precise coordinates of the stone geometry was complicated by the understanding that both the stone and the saw were both wearing, but at different rates. The diamond-tipped saw was also subject to the brute processes of grinding and wearing. The stubborn materiality of the granite registered against the diameter of the saw, causing both to yield. This was eventually addressed by performing a frequent recalibration of the saw to verify its actual dimension and updating the tool pathing appropriately.

As the stone blocks arrived on-site, they were checked against the table for key dimensions. The stone was a Virginia Mist granite with a charcoal gray color and a white feathery vein character. We picked a figured stone to emphasize its three-dimensionality: you can trace the vein figure around the corners of the blocks.

Traditional arches are built with scaffolding and falsework, sequencing assembly from the buttresses to the center with the keystone completing the arch. The precision required of stones at the Sean Collier Memorial necessitated a reverse process. We started with the keystone and worked our way out so that any tolerance was driven outward from the center.

The five-sided irregular keystone was set first, then the five adjacent ring stones were fitted to the keystone. The geometry of the keystone was derived from the irregular angles of the five buttress walls. The faces of the keystone were perpendicular to the thrust vectors of the buttress walls. Each interface between keystone and ring stones consisted of three faces to accommodate a stepped section, resulting in fifteen interfaces that needed to fit together precisely. The keystone and the five ring stones were all supported on scaffolding and built "in the air." Continuous digital surveying allowed for the blocks to be installed "top down."

The erection sequence of working from the inside out reordered the traditional process of working toward the keystone. Because the blocks were transferring loads from block to block, the precise alignment of the stone-to-stone interfaces was critical. Block drawings show the interfaces between blocks, show where load is being transferred from block to block. From the outside we see joint lines, but these are really interfaces, and planes of load transfer.

The joint between stones was only one-quarter-inch wide, which did not allow much room for error—fabrication or erection tolerance.

A precise fit is the only way that the arch actually works; otherwise, there is a risk of the stone joints "opening up." During the construction phase, a team of researchers at MIT applied strain gauges to the joints to measure displacement. The strain gauges effectively turned the built structure into another kind of "model"—in this case, a verification model. This final model—the built structure itself—served as a means to compare the real model against its analytical counterpart and helped us to validate the design process after the fact. In the process of lowering the scaffold, the keystone supports were lowered first. Scales installed under the scaffold allowed MIT researchers to "visualize" the load transfer, from the keystone to the ring stones, and eventually into the buttresses. It is impossible to see force traveling through material. It is possible to measure the shifting of load from center to perimeter during the scaffold removal process. The removal of the scaffold revealed the vaulted figure of the void.

Once the memorial was completed, we were able to appreciate the contrast between the smooth finish of the interior and the

FIGURE 3.3. The Sean Collier Memorial forms a five-way stone vault with buttress walls, forming a new gateway to the MIT campus. Courtesy of Höweler + Yoon, photograph by John Horner.

rough texture of the exterior faces. The concave figure symbolizing "conspicuous absence" is distinctly legible within the memorial, and the low angle of the arch seems to span effortlessly from buttress to buttress.

The completed memorial illustrates a contemporary design workflow, where computational tools for design, analysis, and fabrication are combined into an expanded "document"—the digital model that combines the instruments of service with the tool paths for fabrication, *and* a means of post-occupancy verification. The processes of procurement, fabrication, installation, and erection are incorporated into the documents, creating feedback loops of verification, control, and assurance.

Beyond the scale of a building and the building site, how else might the terms of "verification" and "field" offer insights into designs in which cultural and social contexts delineate the scope and motivation for design? The Memorial to Enslaved Laborers at the University of Virginia involved the precise fabrication and installation of massive blocks of stone. Although the memorial could primarily be perceived as a technical artifact, its impact is felt on a different register, speaking to complex and difficult institutional histories and larger questions of contemporary racism, as well as transforming it into a cultural and political artifact.

The University of Virginia is one of Thomas Jefferson's greatest achievements, and in a sense embodies the ideals associated with American higher education and American democracy. A statue of Jefferson installed on campus depicts Jefferson in the process of surveying the campus. Equipped with a sextant and a topographical survey, Jefferson, the surveyor, the planner, the architect, is depicted as a great visionary, peering into the future to transform "map" into "territory" through the execution of his vision for an "Academical Village."

The UVA "grounds," depicted in an 1830 Tanner Boye engraving, show the ideal campus designed by Jefferson. Ten classically inspired pavilions and a colonnade frame the rotunda. Yet the ideal society that Jefferson envisioned relied on the forced labor of enslaved Africans. The lower left-hand corner of the engraving reveals the basic structure of slavery on which Jefferson's plan relied. An enlargement of the engraving shows an African woman caring for a white child. The forced labor of slavery is hidden in plain sight—embedded in Jefferson's utopian archetype.

A cross-section through the lawn reveals that the two-story pavilions are in fact not two stories high but three. Jefferson's work as land surveyor placed the lawn at the ridgeline of the hill upon which the grounds were built, allowing the rotunda to occupy the highest point and the pavilions to have walk-out basements. The lower level of the pavilion buildings housed spaces for the labor of the enslaved. The spaces behind the pavilions, enclosed by the famous serpentine walls, were work yards where enslaved people chopped wood, hauled water, and slaughtered animals. The institution of slavery is literally *built into* the foundations of the university. Jefferson understood slavery to be abhorrent, and therefore employed architecture and the architectural section to conceal it.

In the process of designing the UVA memorial, we assembled a team of collaborators. Our team included historian and architect Mabel O. Wilson, community engagement specialist and UVA professor Frank Dukes, landscape architect Gregg Bleam, and visual artist Eto Otitigbe. Before we designed anything, we first launched a process of community engagement during which we met and listened to stakeholders from the university, as well as community members, many of whom are descended from the enslaved who worked on the grounds.

Meeting in churches, high school gyms, community centers, and classrooms, we heard many accounts of the generational distrust that members of the community feel toward the university. The grounds are often referred to as "the Plantation." We also heard that for a memorial to be legitimate, it would need to tell the unvarnished truth about the past. The consensus among our interlocutors was that the history of slavery at the university had been covered up: the memorial's job was to acknowledge that history and bring it into the light.

In studying the various proposals and multiple sites on the grounds, we returned to the idea that the memorial should be a place of gathering that would allow people to come together in the present to reflect upon the past. Unlike many monuments that stand as objects in space, the memorial would be a space or a clearing, intended to be occupied and completed by people.

We also learned of an African dance called the "ring shout" in which performers sing and dance in a counterclockwise circle. With this principle in mind, we proposed a clearing and a circular figure as a place of gathering and remembrance.

The geometry of the memorial enters into a dialogue with Jefferson's rotunda: the half sphere of the rotunda's dome is complemented by the bowl-like form of the memorial. The memorial is made up of two cones intersecting slightly off axis, resulting in a tilted figure that emerges from the terrain as the center ring cuts into the ground.

The UVA memorial consists of concentric rings. The outer ring is heavily textured and references the pain and bondage of slavery. The inner ring lists the names of the enslaved. A water feature contains a timeline of the history of slavery at the university, and in the middle is a pristine gathering area planted with grass. A full-scale mock-up in our studio tested the geometry of the memorial

FIGURE 3.4. The Memorial to Enslaved Laborers at the University of Virginia consists of a stone ring embedded in the landscape. Courtesy of Höweler + Yoon, photograph by Alan Karchmer.

relative to the body. Standing with your foot at its base, the slope of the inside wall connects your foot to your outstretched arm, thereby inscribing the body within the geometry of the memorial.

The inner surface of the memorial contains the names of the enslaved. Based on available records, historians have estimated that approximately four thousand enslaved individuals labored on UVA's grounds between 1817 and 1865, although the records are incomplete. Enslaved people were understood as property, so the records contain logs of transactions but often lack basic information such as names. Of the four thousand enslaved, we have 963 individual records, 652 partial names, and only 6 full names.

In translating the names from the records to the wall, we opted to inscribe four thousand marks that work as place holders, each representing an individual. The known names are added to the underscores. We also list occupations, such as farmer or laundress, and kinships, such as mother and daughter. The scarcity of information and the missing names are as powerful as the names themselves.

We recently learned that five new names will be added to the memorial. In this sense the memorial is open-ended: while acknowledging that the records are incomplete, we are hopeful that new scholarship and new DNA tracing will produce more information about these individuals. The cuts in the stone also collect water in the rain, which spills out like tears or like blood from a wound.

The outer surface of the memorial is highly textured, evoking the rough stone textures found on a local gravestone from the same period. Our collaborator, visual artist Eto Otitigbe, worked to develop a pattern that incorporated the textures and traces of the labor of carving stone. Eto's previous work included a piece called *Becoming Visible* in which he photographed himself in a hoodie, in reference to Trayvon Martin, and inscribed his portrait by carving that image into stone. Eto proposed to create a combination of textures for the outer wall of the memorial. The scalloped geometry evokes the rough textures of the gravestones. Overlaid on the scallops are a series of parallel grooves that evoke the textures of rough quarried stone, with tightly spaced drill marks. Embedded within the parallel groves, Eto integrated a photographic image of Isabella Gibbons, a freedwoman, and the subject of one of the few existing photographs of an enslaved person who worked on UVA's grounds.

Eto employed an image-carving technique that translates a raster image into a series of parallel grooves of varying depths. The depth is also related to the width, and the image is mapped onto the scalloped surface. Lastly, the parallel lines are applied to a conical surface. The legibility of the image is highly dependent on the contrasting light as it falls on the grooves. In some light, it is barely detectable. In order to verify the legibility of the technique we tested the groove carving first on scaled stone mockups and then on full scale EPS foam mockups.

The image of Isabella Gibbons is nuanced. Sometimes it is visible, while at other times it is not. This nuance was embedded in the technique of carving the stone and translating the photographic image into the contours of the stone. In some situations the image of Isabella Gibbons is highlighted by shadows and is very visible. At other times, the image is difficult to see.

FIGURE 3.5. The outer wall of the Memorial to Enslaved Laborers is carved to evoke the parallel drill marks of the quarrying process and integrates the image of Isabella Gibbons's eyes. Courtesy of Höweler + Yoon, photograph by Alan Karchmer.

While the Sean Collier Memorial depends on precision for its structural integrity, the UVA memorial depends on precision for its legibility.³ Carving the "raster" grooves into the stone was done with an industrial robot.

In the selection process for a stone fabricator, we asked three pre-qualified fabricators to carve a sample three-by-three-foot stone. We provided the 3D model; they produced the tool paths. After the sample panels were produced, we hired a third party to perform a 3D scan and compared the scan to the original file. Fabricators A and C had several deviations from the 3D model, as much as two-hundredths of an inch. Fabricator B had far fewer deviations from the 3D model. The job was awarded to Fabricator B.

Thinking about precision and contemporary workflows required us to rethink traditional processes of quality assurance and quality control, the checks and balances of fabrication and construction. The promise of digital fabrication does not ensure a desired outcome: what looks acceptable to the naked eye may conceal deviations that are the result of translation from model to tool path.

Shifting from fabrication tolerance to erection tolerance, the process of setting the stone on-site introduced a whole new set of potentials for error, a new set of understandings of precision, and the need for field verification. In setting stones on-site, the stones are located in space via digital surveying equipment, supported on shims, and eventually backfilled with grout after the geometry is confirmed.

One of the challenges of architecture is balancing the relation of "part to whole." Even when an architectural form is conceived as a monolithic ring, the implementation in the field implies multiple parts coming together to form that singular line. The UVA memorial relies on the ridgeline to create the new "horizon" within which the contemplative space of the memorial takes shape. Comparing construction photos to images of the 3D model shows the striking resemblance and the highly accurate continuity of the ridgeline. Experiencing the memorial produces an uncanny effect. The memorial is material, massive, and made up of distinct parts, but at the same time it looks like something that flickered across our computer screens for months leading up to the construction.

During the construction process, the alignment of the individual stones was additive. Each stone followed the previous stone, until the figure was completed. But the geometrical operation that produced the digital file during the design process was subtractive, a Rhino 3D operation referred to as "Boolean difference": subtracting one geometry from another. How the parts and the joints that they form come together is of critical importance. The joint at the ridgeline shows two panels coming together: the smooth interior and the rough exterior. The two meet at a "quirk miter." The knife-edge was blunted to avoid breakage. The gap in between was filled with a backer rod and silicone caulk. Looking at the finished memorial along the continuous ridgeline, the built structure appears eerily familiar, as if you were in the presence of something that has escaped the digital and is present in the real world.

How was the stone aligned to create this continuity? A number of hydraulic jacks lifted the stone into position while a digital surveyor verified that the points in space conformed to the digital model. The effect has the appearance of a monolith, even though we know it is made up of many parts, perfectly aligned.

Like the Sean Collier Memorial, the UVA memorial relies on the interfaces between discrete parts. In this case, the faces are not transferring forces, but their alignments are essential to the monolithic reading and the legibility of the colossal eyes.

The memorial allows the viewer to measure the body against its geometries. Views from the exterior highlight the landform qualities that contrast the smooth interior with the rough exterior, and recall the traces of the digital, casting shadows in the real.

The construction of the UVA memorial involved high degrees of precision and processes of testing, measuring, validating, and verifying. It also unearthed painful histories. The completed memorial has been embraced by many in the community, and UVA has acknowledged its impact in the rebuilding of trust with the community. The "field of work," in this case, is bound up in history and in processes of recognition and reconciliation.

As we expand our understanding of design to include the broader contexts in which we work, the labor that has gone into their assembly, the communities they affect, and the environment that they become a part of, it is useful to think of "building" as a noun as well as a verb. The process of building involves flows of materials, labor, energy, and waste. The building itself, the noun, is just a moment in a much larger process. Architect Kiel Moe describes the physical building as an "isolated object-instance" within a much larger network of linkages, processes, and flows of materials and labor.[4]

The last project to be discussed is an inhabitable sculpture located in Spokane, Washington, on the site of the former 1974 World's Fair. In this case, the structure, called the Timber Stepwell, is conceived as an instrument for looking and surveying the site. The diagonal cut through the sculpture opens up a sight line across the landscape to another sculpture.

The site is quite dramatic, with gorges and waterfalls that historically were part of the Spokane tribe's hunting and fishing grounds and eventually became part of the development of Spokane's mill and hydroelectric power industries.

Initial studies highlighted alignments across the site's topography and the potential for multiple pavilions to be sited relative to their sight lines. We also wanted to draw attention to the history of logging in the Pacific Northwest and the use of wood as a basic raw material that was associated with the place.

Evaluating the environmental aspects of a building today requires that we take into account energy performance, as well as its material and embodied energy footprint. As architects, the agency in specifying a material or a system is one of the most significant decisions that we make in the design of a building.

By specifying wood as a construction material, instead of steel or concrete, we chose to avoid the energy expenditures of such high-energy practices as extraction and processing. Building with renewable materials, such as mass timber, has other benefits, including carbon sequestration and impacts on land uses and forestry practices.

As part of our research into mass timber as a building system, we proposed Stepwell, a public art installation in Spokane, as a stacked mass timber structure. Understood as a device for looking, the Stepwell project points beyond itself, with a diagonal sightline that bisects the plan and a lookout platform at both ends of the structure. The exterior is sloped to accentuate the cantilevered form; the interior profile is terraced for seating. The nonparallel faces of the interior and the exterior suggest the use of material as volume—one no longer composed of beams and planes.

FIGURE 3.6. The Stepwell project forms a sculptural pavilion at the site of Spokane's Riverfront Park. Courtesy of Höweler + Yoon.

The mass timber industry is evolving beyond the traditional techniques of framing and sheathing as it embraces the scale of engineered lumber well beyond the dimensions of wood sources, namely the size of the trunk. Engineered wood takes advantage of glues and composites, which reconfigure wood to improve yields and use components of varying qualities. However, the mass timber industry is primarily focused on cutting flat sheets and beams, relying on sheets cut in planar configurations, perpendicular to the surface. A multi-axis industrial robot is capable of a far more three-dimensional work envelope, which allows it to cut volumetric elements, such as blocks of stone.

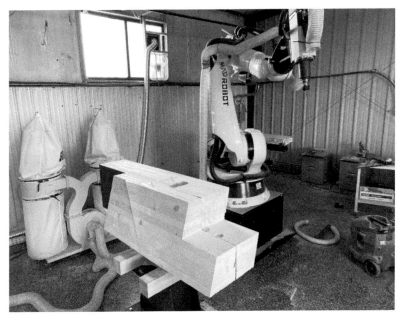

FIGURE 3.7. The glue-laminated mass timber blocks are carved with a multi-axis robot to use the timber in a volumetric way. Courtesy of Quarra Stone Company.

For the Stepwell project, we began testing the work envelope of a robotic mill to carve truly massive mass timber elements. Rather than substituting conventional building elements with alternative renewable materials, we opted for a structure that was inherently volumetric and used the mass of the mass timber to implement it.

The Stepwell project consists of seventy blocks of stacked glue laminated tiers of Alaska Yellow Cedar. Components fabricated in the shop as volumetric blocks were then transported to the site and erected in large pieces. Maximizing the size of blocks reduces the field labor and relies on the precision of a shop fabrication environment. Optimization involved making repeating blocks that stack to produce the Stepwell geometry, and erection sequences showed the process of assembling large volumetric parts to form the singular "whole."

Each species of wood has unique properties, including grain character, pest resistance, weathering characteristics, and expansion due to moisture content. Alaska Yellow Cedar was selected in part because of its weathering characteristics. It is expected to weather into a silvery gray.

Like all works of architecture, construction involves the assembling of discrete "parts" into a singular "whole." How those parts fit together is key, as every joint is an interface of force, alignment, and expansion or contraction. Minimizing joints allows for more control and less field contingency.

The completed structure produces a monolithic interior, scaled to the body and to ergonomic proportions, that is distinct from its exterior appearance. By constructing the sculpture from solid blocks of timber, we sought to create a unique structure that recalls the material history of the place while speculating on new uses for mass timber products.

The volumetric use of mass timber to form the steps and walls of the Stepwell project suggests monolithic construction more akin to masonry construction. The "blocks" of mass timber resemble corbeling in stone. The design of Timber Stepwell applies experiences gained from the use of volumetric stone at the Sean Collier Memorial, where the fabrication envelope of a robotic mill was employed to arrive at a solution that was inherently volumetric. We understand Stepwell as a stereotomic mass that produces spatial and structural configurations analogous to vaults and shells rather than frames and skins. Using mass timber in a truly volumetric way reveals new expressive potential for engineered wood not simply as a substitute for steel and concrete but as an alternative to previous construction modes, or what critic Elisa Iturbe would call "carbon modernity."[5]

To find alternatives to carbon form requires prototyping new modes of carbon sequestering, rapidly renewable building materials that offer new possibilities. An accounting of the embodied energy of projects such as Stepwell offers alternative material flows and energy footprints. Thinking through material, its qualities and quantities, procurement and processes, allows us to imagine an approach to building with the earth in mind, in line with what philosopher Bruno Latour qualifies as an "earthly account of building,"[6] an architecture of accountability.

The translation from drawing to building, from concept to construction, is never a linear process, despite our embrace of digital tools and fabrication techniques. In construction, there is ample room for friction, gaps for tolerance and deflection, and anticipated and unanticipated conditions that require the feedback implicit in the verify in field notation.

In each case, the field conditions, constraints, motivations, and materials are different, but the strategies for working back and forth across the boundaries of conception and construction, between design intent and means and methods, community and climate, have been instrumental. Strategies for verification, integration, and tolerance become drivers for design, where materials and methods, engagement, and environment imprint themselves on the apparent seamlessness of our digital design processes.

Our contemporary use of digital tools, whether 3D modeling or cutting stone with a robotic saw, all work through media. In our practice, we have shifted from arguing for expanding the field by including "media as a material" to contemplating the status of "material after media."

The Cold War quip "trust but verify," attributed to Ronald Reagan in the context of Cold War détente, implies a direct assertion that truth can be verified. Either there were missiles in the silos, or there were not. Writing in 2020, a common understanding of a shared reality, a shared understanding of truth, and the articulation of common values seems increasingly remote. It is paradoxical that the age of "post-truth" coincides with the Information Age, the age of big data and of peak knowledge. Yet the need for verification through systems of feedback, and techniques for translation, has never been more urgent.

NOTES

1 Robin Evans has pointed out that architects do not make buildings but drawings of buildings. See Robin Evans, "Translations from Drawing to Building," *Translations from Drawings to Buildings, and Other Essays* (Cambridge, MA: MIT Press, 1997). Mario Carpo has updated the discussion around drawing to focus on digital drawings. See Mario Carpo, *The Second Digital Turn* (Cambridge, MA: MIT Press, 2017).

2 Francesca Hughes, *The Architecture of Error: Matter, Measure, and the Misadventures of Precision* (Cambridge, MA: MIT Press, 2014), 5.

3 The discussion of "precision" in a volume on "exactitude" deserves some

mention. "Precision" is more commonly used in day-to-day discussions of dimensions, specifications, and tolerance. "Exactitude" is distinct from "exactness" and is less commonly used. In the realm of architectural notation, a specific dimension string may be labeled as "hold," meaning this dimension is critical, and if necessary, other dimensions might be subject to adjustment. Exactitude might be an ideal principle, something to be aspired to but rarely achieved. Precision seems to allow for *degrees* of precision, including room for error. I used the term "precision" in my essay, but I may have actually been talking about "exactitude."

4 Kiel Moe, *Empire, State & Building* (New York: Actar, 2017), 19.

5 Elisa Iturbe, "Architecture and the Death of Carbon Modernity," *Log 47* (Fall 2019): 11

6 "Only by generating earthly accounts of buildings and design processes, tracing pluralities of concrete entities in the specific spaces and times of their co-existence, instead of referring to abstract theoretical frameworks outside architecture, will architectural theory become a relevant field for architects, for end users, for promoters, and for builders." Bruno Latour and Albena Yaneva, "'Give Me a Gun and I Will Make All Buildings Move': An Ant's View of Architecture," in *Explorations in Architecture, Teaching Design Research,* ed. Reto Geiser (Basel: Birkhäuser, 2008), 88.

EXACTITUDE ADRIFT

Chapter 4

Exactitude and the Weather

Christopher Benfey

> Please don't talk to me about the weather. Whenever people talk to me about the weather, I always feel that they mean something else.
> —Gwendolen, in Oscar Wilde's *The Importance of Being Earnest*

"I have been listening to Mozart," the old physicist said, as he welcomed us into his split-level house in Greensboro, North Carolina. He had an LP, a red Columbia vinyl disc, on the record player. It was one of the late piano concertos. We all stopped for a moment in the living room, taking in the music. This happened forty years ago. I don't remember the physicist's name. I don't remember what we ate. But I do remember my impression of the music. It was sumptuous, like red velvet, but also precise, with a mathematical elegance. The music, the slowly revolving disc, the rectangular spaces of the house all suggested an intricate structure, as though the music was somehow erecting a shelter around us in the stormy night. I remember one other thing from that evening. It was something the old physicist said. The weather had come up, the subject people talk about when there's nothing else to talk about. What the old physicist said that turbulent night in Greensboro was this: "Meteorology is not an exact science."

The old physicist's remark about the limits of meteorology was not original; a Google search identifies it as an "old adage," so familiar and widely used that no source is given. But it was new to me. And what made it memorable was the confluence of two forces: the intricacy and exactitude of Mozart and the imprecision of meteorology. Or, to give the opposition another name, exactitude and the weather. I want to assemble some evidence that it is difficult, perhaps impossible, to come to grips with the notion of exactitude without wrestling with its various opposites, its discontents. It may even be the case that the quest for exactitude invites its opposites onto the scene, like the uninvited guest in a fairy tale.

High on the list of these enemies of exactitude, at least as far as architecture is concerned, is the weather.[1] No matter how precisely the building plans are drawn on paper, or on the computer screen, weather has a way of making itself a conspicuous—if a generally uninvited—part of the proceedings. "The Life of Buildings in Time" is how Mohsen Mostafavi and David Leatherbarrow subtitled their 1993 book *On Weathering*. The implication is that however ideally—with whatever imagined exactitude—buildings exist in space, they must also exist in time, and hence in a world of incessant change, and even mortality. It is within that radically unideal realm of time and change that the weather works its menace. "In architecture," Mostafavi and Leatherbarrow write, "the gradual destruction of buildings by nature in time is weathering."[2]

In an era of rapid climate change like our own, we may have to modify their formulation about the destruction of buildings by nature in time. How quaint it sounds, looking back from our vantage point in 2021, to refer to the *gradual* destruction of buildings by nature. In her recent book, *The Ruins Lesson,* the poet and literary critic Susan Stewart goes deeply into the question of buildings destroyed over time. Stewart moves beyond the customary analysis of the cultural taste for ruins, in, for example, Giovanni Battista Piranesi and William Wordsworth, arguing instead that all artistic creation is built, in some sense, on the ruins of the past. Contemporary sonnets are built from the ruins of previous sonnets. On the topic of weather, Stewart stresses not gradual change but violent, drastic, immediate change. "Persons and things can be slowly ruined by suffering the depredations of use and ordinary weather,"

Stewart writes, "and in times of violence and extreme weather, they can be actively ruined."[3] Welcome to extreme weather, she seems to say—fires and floods, tornadoes and hurricanes—our present and our future.

One strategy adopted by architects faced with extreme weather —especially in the postindustrial era, with its premium on permanency and interchangeable, precision-made parts—has been to develop ever more weather-resistant materials: stainless steel, reinforced glass, protective paints, and so on. We might think of this as an architecture of climate-change denial. A very different strategy, especially among architects more attuned to particular regions, local resources, and site-specific building practices, has been to embrace the natural effects of weathering over time, to allow for them, to welcome them, and even to plan for them.[4] For if there is menace in weathering, especially in extreme weathering, there can also be magic. A major aim of Mostafavi and Leatherbarrow's monograph is to recover a positive contribution from the weather, to view what time does to a building as occasionally, and even in certain cases deliberately, an enhancement rather than a diminution. "In the mathematics of the environment," they write, "weathering is a power of subtraction, a *minus,* under the sign of which newly finished corners, surfaces, and colors are 'taken away' by rain, wind, and sun. But is weathering only subtraction, can it not also *add* and enhance? . . . Creation in this sense is the work of an architect and builder anticipating the work of the elements."[5] Time and the weather are thus brought into the act of creation, as invited guests and collaborators.

Architects are hardly alone among material-based artists and designers in anticipating the contributions, rather than just the destructive powers, of climate activity. In fact, whole aesthetic systems, like the Japanese concept of *wabi* (that active embrace of the transient and the imperfect) or the picturesque taste for dilapidated walls or decayed thatched cottages that flourished in nineteenth-century Europe, can be based on aesthetic partnership with weathering and time.[6] Even whole art forms, like wood-fired ceramics, arise from a deliberately contrived confluence of the ancient natural elements of earth, air, fire, and water. The wood-fired kiln introduces the quintessential fifth element of chance, producing those invited accidents that are the glory of much Japanese pottery associated with the tea ceremony. Such seemingly weathered objects exist in deliberate contrast to the apparent permanency of fine porcelain. The whole process of creating wood-fired ceramics is like an allegory of surviving and thriving amid the violent and unpredictable vicissitudes of climate change.

It is particularly interesting to see the opposition of exactitude and the weather emerging in aesthetic traditions in which a high finish of craftsmanship and precision is treasured and even demanded. A striking example is the Japanese novelist Jun'ichirō Tanizaki's beautiful essay on Japanese aesthetics, *In Praise of Shadows* (1933–34). In his attempt to define a distinctively Asian aesthetic in contrast to supposed Western values of clarity, direct light, and stainless steel, Tanizaki evokes the high finish of Asian craftsmen and architects, working in lacquer and jade, before zeroing in on his real interest: what time and the weather do to human artifacts. "We do love things that bear the marks of grime, soot, and weather," he writes, "and we love the colors and the sheen that call to mind the past that made them."[7] In this case, "the past" refers both to the human makers and to the by turns destructive and aesthetically enhancing work of time.

This Japanese love of the stained, the damaged, and the imperfect goes back centuries, to writings by the fourteenth-century court official and Buddhist monk known as Kenkō, whose *Essays in Idleness* define, like Tanizaki, a combination of exact workmanship and damage. "Somebody once remarked," Kenkō writes, "that thin silk was not satisfactory as a scroll wrapping because it was so easily torn." To which he replies, "It is only after the silk wrapper has frayed at top and bottom, and the mother-of-pearl has fallen from the roller that a scroll looks beautiful." Kenkō quotes another authority who wrote, "Even when building the imperial palace, they always leave one place unfinished."[8] The Buddhist tolerance of evanescence is evident in these passages, of course. But perhaps there is a more subtle aversion to the perfected, the complete, the exact.

For me, the most beautiful invocation of this aversion to perfection comes from the American poet Wallace Stevens. I am thinking of "The Poems of Our Climate," a short poem from 1942. The title of the poem explicitly evokes the weather. Stevens, whom Calvino in his "Exactitude" memo categorizes as a poet of crystalline precision,[9] begins with an image of perfection, of exactitude: pink and white carnations in a porcelain bowl of "clear water, brilliant-edged."[10] An assiduous student of Asian aesthetics, Stevens identifies exactitude with coldness:[11] The light in the room is "like a snowy air, reflecting snow"; the porcelain, that material of crystalline perfection, is "cold." The enemies of exactitude, by contrast, are summoned from our own hotter emotional needs. Stevens's ending to "The Poems of Our Climate" is another hymn to imperfection in the Japanese mode. "The imperfect," he writes, "is our paradise." For Stevens, who spent his life in New England, weather is both metaphor and reality. In "The Poems of Our Climate," perfection is identified with winter, a crystalline coldness indistinguishable from death. In such a world, heat is life: "the imperfect is so *hot* in us."

Italo Calvino already foresaw this dialectic of exactitude and its opposites in the text from which this volume draws its theme. "Every concept and value turns out to be double," he writes, "even exactitude." Calvino then quotes a passage from his novel *Invisible Cities* that would seem the very essence of geometric exactitude, an evocation of a game of chess. But it is weather and weathering that takes over. "Your chessboard," Marco Polo observes, "is inlaid with two woods: ebony and maple. The square on which your enlightened gaze is fixed was cut from the ring of a trunk that grew in a year of drought: you see how its fibers are arranged? Here a barely hinted knot can be made out: a bud tried to burgeon on a premature spring day, but the night's frost forced it to desist."[12]

The "barely hinted knot" evoked in this oblique passage invites wider speculation regarding the relation of precision and its enemies. Two other literary figures, both of whom are explicitly invoked in Calvino's "Exactitude" memo, address ramifications of the conflict. One is the French poet, essayist, and mathematician Paul Valéry. The other is the American writer Edgar Allan Poe. "In our century," Calvino writes, "Paul Valéry is the one who has best defined poetry as a straining after exactitude." Calvino traces a "poetics of exactitude" in a straight line from Valéry back to his master, Stéphane Mallarmé, then further back to Charles Baudelaire, and finally to Baudelaire's own great predecessor, Edgar Allan Poe. In Poe, as Calvino notes, Valéry saw "le démon de la lucidité," the demon of lucidity, and "the literary engineer who studied and utilized all the resources of art."[13]

Poe famously claimed, in his essay "The Philosophy of Composition," that at no point in the writing of his poem "The Raven" was anything left to "accident or intuition." Instead, Poe insists, "the work proceeded, step by step, to its completion, with the precision and rigid consequence of a mathematical problem."[14] It is this side of Poe that so appealed to Paul Valéry, who abandoned poetry for twenty years to pursue his mathematical interests. It is also the side of Poe that appeals to Calvino.

And yet—in a familiar pattern—the search for exactitude in Poe's poems and stories seems inevitably to summon its opposite, the workings of time and the weather. These themes in Poe's work seem to arise from some repressed region of the mind, or of the climate. Here one might suggest that the proper literary mode of weathering is in fact the Gothic, the mode for which Poe is best known. I am thinking here of Poe's lurid story of Gothic horror, creepy doppelgängers, incest, and architecture, "The Fall of the House of Usher." I wish to tease out just one thematic thread from the preposterously complex weave of the story, namely, the tension between exactitude and its opposites, specifically in relation to architecture. Roderick Usher, seemingly the sole occupant of his moldering, hereditary palace until his mortally ill sister and identical twin—indeed, his exact replica—appears on the scene, is portrayed as a demon of lucidity, given to mathematical calculations, fantastical architectural designs, and the intricacies of music.

Usher, we are informed, is an artist and a designer of abstract spaces, "phantasmagoric conceptions," as the narrator refers to them, most conspicuously of a great underground vault destined, apparently, for his sister's entombment. "A small picture presented the interior of an immensely long and rectangular vault or tunnel, with low walls, smooth, white, and without interruption or device." No source of light is discernible. But as in those ghostly interiors of the artist James Turrell or the architect Tadao Ando, "a flood of intense rays rolled throughout and bathed the whole in a ghastly and inappropriate splendor."[15]

The house in which Usher lives, the famous House of Usher itself, shows the marks of what time does to architectural designs.

"Its principal feature seemed to be that of an excessive antiquity," Poe's narrator remarks of the house. "The discoloration of ages had been great."[16] Minute fungi cover the exterior. And yet, there is a certain aesthetic clash in the appearance of the house. Twice, Poe invokes "inconsistency" as a key feature of the house's design. "No portion of the masonry had fallen; and there appeared to be a wild inconsistency between its still perfect adaptation of parts, and the utterly porous, and evidently decayed condition of the individual stones."[17] Here, we can discern that same tension between exactitude—in its "still perfect adaptation of parts"—and the weather, with its stain and decay. In Roderick Usher himself, the doomed musical prodigy and fantastical architect, the narrator discerns a kindred inconsistency: "In the manner of my friend I was at once struck with an incoherence—an inconsistency; and I soon found this to arise from a series of feeble and futile struggles to overcome an habitual trepidancy, an excessive nervous agitation."[18]

The word "inconsistency" is a reminder that Calvino's final, unwritten lecture was to be about the aesthetic concept of consistency. There is a certain charm, a fitting ending, in this missing sixth memo for the next millennium, the millennium in which we have already lived for twenty years. In this regard, Calvino may be considered a kindred spirit of the fourteenth-century Buddhist priest Kenkō, who invoked the imperial palace in which one portion is left unfinished. "In both Buddhist and Confucian writings of former times," Kenkō adds, "there are also many missing chapters."[19]

I want to conclude by circling back to Paul Valéry, the poet who, according to Calvino, "best defined poetry as a straining after exactitude."[20] In 1921, Valéry published a remarkable essay on architecture, in the form of a Socratic dialogue, called "Eupalinos, or The Architect." The essay has come to have a certain weight of finality in the history of modernism for two reasons. A German translation of the essay was the last major work of the poet Rainer Maria Rilke. And a preface to the English translation of Valéry's essay was the last major work of Wallace Stevens.[21]

"Eupalinos" is set in the afterworld, as Socrates and his younger friend Phaedrus debate the essence of architecture. Socrates associates architecture with music, as two essentially nonmimetic arts that, as he puts it, "borrow a minimum from natural objects." The linkage of architecture to music is of course longstanding and complex, reaching back to Pythagoras.[22] Le Corbusier suggestively described the Parthenon as a "brazen trumpet" and consistently invoked what one architectural historian has described as the "acoustical trope" in his writings.[23] Similarly, twice in the essay Valéry's two speakers take up the question of how a building can "sing," suggesting some unheard melody—some shared structural principle—linking architecture and music beyond the merely metaphorical.[24] And Socrates, reversing the metaphor, describes music as "a mobile edifice"—in French "un édifice mobile."[25] As they cast about for a perfect example of music as architecture, and architecture as music, Phaedrus quotes extensively from an acquaintance, a master-architect named Eupalinos. Eupalinos's quintessential building, itself a "mobile edifice," is in fact a ship.

And it is precisely here, in Valéry's dialectical scheme, that meteorology enters the picture. For Eupalinos's ship, in its quest for "lastingness," is so closely congruent with the weather, with the climatic forces, that it essentially *becomes* the weather. "He would passionately imagine the natures of the winds and the waters," Phaedrus says of Eupalinos," the mobility and the resistance of their fluids. He would ponder upon the birth of tempests and calms, the circulation of warm currents . . . he would consider the whims and veerings of the breezes." Eupalinos, he adds, "thought that a ship should, in some sort, be created by the knowledge of the sea, and should almost be fashioned by the very wave itself."[26] One can see emerging here a familiar theme in twentieth-century architectural discourse, first enunciated by Louis Sullivan, that form follows function.[27] "It sometimes used to seem to me that an impression of beauty was born of exactitude," Phaedrus remarks, "and that a sort of delight was engendered by the almost miraculous conformity of an object with the function that it must fulfill."[28]

But what I take from Valéry's essay is a more radical insight, a leap from his notion of music as a "mobile edifice" to a vision of a truly mobile architecture. For at the heart of his essay lies an inkling that the future of the human race (and of the planet on which we live) lies in mobility, and in "mobile edifices" that take their promptings from wind and wave. In this spirit, we may think of a bold experiment such as the 2002 Blur Building by the architectural firm of Diller Scofidio+Renfro, in which a deliberately ephemeral structure of primarily water vapor was erected above a lake in Switzerland.[29] The weather, in Valéry's vision, is no longer an enemy to be outflanked by ever more resistant materials. Instead, it is seen as a necessary partner, an inspiration, in our architectural endeavors. Our homes have always been, in a sense, mobile homes, perched precariously on this spinning planet racing through space. But Valéry implies that they will have to be even more closely adapted to the weather, eventually becoming, like Eupalinos's ship, the wind and waves themselves.

To vary the quote attributed to Gandhi: we ourselves must be the change that we want to see in the world, including climate change. If there is to be any "lastingness" in these perilous times, for us and for our planet, our edifices must even more perfectly partake of the unpredictable vicissitudes of climate. In the face of climate change, the ravages of time, and the shortness of available time, are consistently on our minds. We must strive for exactitude in our data and in our forecasts, but also—if we are to survive—for creative accommodation: with time and the weather.

For as the old physicist told me forty years ago, meteorology is not an exact science.

NOTES

1 To revise Wilde, in my epigraph, whenever we talk about exactitude, we must also talk about the weather. See Oscar Wilde, *The Importance of Being Earnest* (New York: Dover, 2012), 10.

2 Mohsen Mostafavi and David Leatherbarrow, *On Weathering: The Life of Buildings in Time* (Cambridge, MA: MIT Press, 1993), 6.

3 Susan Stewart, *The Ruins Lesson: Meaning and Material in Western Culture* (Chicago, IL: University of Chicago Press, 2020), 1.

4 See Kenneth Frampton, "Towards a Critical Regionalism: Six Points for an Architecture of Resistance," in *The Anti-Aesthetic: Essays on Post-Modern Culture,* ed. Hal Foster (Seattle, WA: Bay Press, 1983), 21: "The fundamental strategy of Critical Regionalism is to mediate the impact of universal civilization with elements derived indirectly from the peculiarities of a particular place. . . . It may find its governing inspiration in such things as the range and quality of the local light, or in a tectonic derived from a peculiar structural mode, or in the topography of a given site."

5 Mostafavi and Leatherbarrow, *On Weathering,* 39.

6 For a classic account of the Japanese taste for impermanence and the imperfect, see Kakuzo Okakura, *The Book of Tea*, edited by Christopher Benfey (New York: Penguin, 2010). A still relevant formulation of the taste for dilapidation can be found in Georg Simmel's essay "The Ruin," translated by David Kettler, in *Hudson Review* 11, no. 3 (Autumn 1958): 379–85. "It is the fascination of the ruin," Simmel argues, "that here the work of man appears to us entirely as a product of nature. The same forces which give a mountain its shape through weathering, erosion, faulting, growth of vegetation, here do their work on old walls" (381).

7 Jun'ichirō Tanizaki, *In Praise of Shadows*, trans. Thomas J. Harper and Edward G. Seidensticker (Stony Creek, CT: Leete's Island Books, 1977), 11.

8 Kenkō, *Essays in Idleness*, trans. Donald Keene (New York: Columbia University Press, 1967), 70, 71. Kenkō (sometimes referred to as Yoshida Kenkō) denounces "the practice of deliberately building in a tasteless and ugly manner 'to keep the house from showing its age'" (70).

9 Italo Calvino, *Six Memos for the Next Millennium*, trans. Patrick Creagh (New York: Vintage, 1993), 70. "The emblem of crystal," Calvino writes, "might be used to distinguish a whole constellation of poets and writers," among which he includes, among others, the French poet Paul Valéry and the Argentine writer Jorge Luis Borges.

10 Wallace Stevens, "The Poems of Our Climate," in *The Collected Poems of Wallace Stevens* (New York: Vintage, 1990), 193.

11 Stevens studied the writings of the Japanese art historian Kakuzō Okakura, author of *The Book of Tea* (1906). For Stevens's interest in Asian aesthetics, see Christopher Benfey, *The Great Wave: Gilded Age Misfits, Japanese Eccentrics, and the Opening of Old Japan* (New York: Random House, 2003), 76, 103, 106.

12 Calvino, *Six Memos*, 72, 73.

13 Ibid., 67.

14 Edgar Allan Poe, "The Philosophy of Composition" (1846), in Poe, *Essays and Reviews*, ed. G. R. Thompson (New York: Library of America, 1984), 15.

15 Edgar Allan Poe, "The Fall of the House of Usher," in Poe, *Poetry and Tales*, ed. Patrick F. Quinn (New York: Library of America, 1984), 325.

16 Poe, *Poetry and Tales*, 319.

17 Ibid.

18 Ibid., 321.

19 Kenkō, *Essays in Idleness*, 71.

20 Calvino, *Six Memos*, 67.

21 Paul Valéry, *Dialogues*, trans. William McCausland Stewart (Princeton, NJ: Princeton University Press, 1956). In the first of two prefaces to this volume, Stevens writes, "Rilke read *Eupalinos* when it came out in the *Nouvelle Revue française*, and his translation of it was the last work he did before he died" (xxi). Of the two prefaces, Stewart writes, "They are, 'except, perhaps, for a poem or two,' says his literary executor Samuel French Morse, 'Stevens's last significant work'" (193).

22 Ibid., 99. The comparison of architecture and music is not original with Valéry. In his early work *Nature*, Emerson attributes it to both Goethe and Madame de Staël. "Thus, architecture is called 'frozen music,' by De Staël and Goethe. Vitruvius thought an architect should be a musician." Ralph Waldo Emerson, *Essays and Lectures*, edited by Joel Porte (New York: Library of America, 1983), 30.

23 See Christopher Pearson, "Le Corbusier and the Acoustical Trope: An Investigation of Its Origins," *Journal of the Society of Architectural Historians* 56 (1997): 168–83. "The better-known use of this metaphor in reference to the Parthenon occurs again in *Vers une architecture*, where Le Corbusier describes the temples on the Acropolis as 'closely-knit and violent elements, sounding clear and tragic like brazen trumpets'" (196).

24 Valéry, *Dialogues,* 83, 93.

25 Ibid., 94, 102.

26 Ibid., 137.

27 Louis Sullivan, "The Tall Office Building Artistically Considered," in *Lippincott's Magazine* (March 1896): 408: "Whether it be the sweeping eagle in his flight, or the open apple-blossom, the toiling workhorse, the blithe swan, the branching oak, the winding stream at its base, the drifting clouds, over all the coursing sun, form ever follows function, and this is the law."

28 Valéry, *Dialogues*, 129.

29 Built for the Swiss Expo 2002, the structure was dismantled after the exposition closed. See https://www.designingbuildings.co.uk/wiki/Blur_ Building. The architects referred to the Blur Building as an "architecture of atmosphere," a phrase that resonates with the title of Silvia Benedito's recent *Atmosphere Anatomies: On Design, Weather, and Sensation* (Zurich: Lars Müller Publishers, 2020).

FIGURE 5.1. Mizuta Museum of Art north facade. Courtesy studioSUMO.

Chapter 5
Building in the Floating World

Sunil Bald

I would like to examine exactitude through floating. Not in opposition to it, though the shape of the words couldn't be more different. "Exactitude" has a menacing staccato sharpness; it feels like a dangerous word, one that could puncture the gentle roundness of floating and bring it down to earth at any moment. "Exactitude" also emanates an assuredness in its linearity—a prefigured intention awaiting accurate and measurable realization. "Floating," on the other hand, adapts its course in response to forces and winds from multiple directions, relieved from the burden of destination. In this chapter, I would like to explore how the clarity of ideas and architectural objects result from an indeterminant and nonlinear process that bends to the unpredictability of events and collaboration.

In his essay "Exactitude," Italo Calvino argues for precision in writing, from outline (or prefiguration) to image to detail.[1] This precision relies on shared evocation through the consensus of shared language. In building, one might translate this into a shared ground from which, and on which, to measure, to outline. This can extend to a shared sense of "groundedness" in which architecture strives to conjure a sense of being in and belonging to the social context of its siting.

To "float" is to be denied access, to be outside, to be ungrounded. While this may create a sense of crisis in the modern Western psyche, floating inspires more complex states of being going back to Taoism, to which, according to the art historian David Waterhouse, the origins of the term "floating world" can be traced.[2] The concept of the floating world in Buddhist texts from tenth-century Japan could also mean "sad, troublesome world" or "going with the flow." The lotus, a common subject in Japanese literature and art of the time, reflects the floating Buddha. With its roots in an earth that is liquid, muddy, and without the stability or orientation of a datum, or ground, it cannot inhabit, settle, or even lay out the critical dimensions for a building foundation. Perhaps Calvino's evocation of clarity is embodied not by the lotus roots but by the lotus flower, delineated against the sky, a kind of floating where purpose is not something rooted but an aspiration that one pursues.

An image of the floating flower by the seventeenth-century Japanese artist Ogata Kōrin leads me to briefly describe ukiyo-e, commonly translated as "pictures of the floating world," as a portal into the ideas and experiences that informed the work of studioSUMO in Japan over a fifteen-year period. Frequently, all Japanese woodblock prints are grouped together as ukiyo-e. However, the word originally referred to something very specific that developed around the growth of Edo, the city that became Tokyo, where power was consolidated after the fall of the regional shogunate, and the seeds of the Japanese nation were planted. As the scholar Timon Screech has noted, calligraphy and woodcut prints in early Edo were typically meant to document and idealize everyday life in a growing metropolis for a protected elite whose movement was restricted.[3] Calligraphy might recount the time the rooster crowed in the morning or how many bags of rice were delivered, while images such as Hokusai's print showing a new bridge over the Sumida River celebrated the technical prowess and infrastructure of the new city. In short, these images crafted a master narrative of an idealized city for a fixed audience that was protected from the complexities of burgeoning urbanity by their social stature. Fixity became paradigmatic to central Edo, regulated by social hierarchy and reinforced in images.

With the growth of urban culture and a new type of nonagrarian work, however, came a new type of leisure, that of commodified entertainment. The shogunate sanctioned spaces for such activities but removed them from the fixed world, in the case of Edo, creating the Yoshiwara District north of the center, up the Sumida River from the temple district of Asukasa, which was then the northern edge of Edo. Being thus removed, the area became rich with burgeoning theater, geisha houses, and brothels. To keep the fun from getting out of hand, on entering the district, men were required to check their swords, which denoted their social rank. Removed from the fixed world and one's place in it, Yoshiwara became known as the floating world, ukiyo, and the pictures that idealized its actors, courtesans, and spaces as ukiyo-e. And idealized they were, for the images obscured the violence and sexual slavery within.[4]

Sharaku, one of the most renowned ukiyo-e artists, was himself a floating being. Executing some of the best-known portraits of his time, Sharaku appeared out of nowhere in March 1794 and disappeared ten months later, his whole artistic production, 142 images being completed in that span of time. Yoshiwara's or Sharaku's existence (or nonexistence) offers an understanding of floating that challenges fixity and groundedness, rather than against exactitude. Indeed, the floating world had its own protocols of precision. The ukiyo-e of Hishikawa Moronobu titled *Tsubone agarau to mo* depicts a low-end brothel in Yoshiwara, with the display room on the left and the private room behind the orange curtain on the right. Within the word that describes the brothel, *Tsubone,* is *tsubo,* which to this day remains the unit of measure for floor area in Japan, equal to two tatami mats or 3.3 square meters, quantifying the space and consequently equating the experience of encounter with exactitude.

Floating Practice

Now I will veer sharply toward architectural practice to explore the fluid relationship of measures and numbers to the circumstances, sometimes ephemeral or even accidental, that are encountered in architectural practice. While the space between architectural intention as drawn and architectural object as built might be measurable, even quantifiable, by objective or subjective criteria, architectural practice floats between multiple forces, ambitions, preconceptions, and expectations, which can each have their own form of exactitude, sometimes an arbitrary exactitude, and be guided by a collection of measures that are exemplified by two projects from our practice at studioSUMO. Both were modest in scope but demanding in navigating the values and numbers that influenced their flow toward realization.

Looking at studioSUMO's series of projects in Japan from 2003 to 2018, our practice can be epitomized as an exercise in floating. Having recently been formed, SUMO had little access to the fixed world of architectural opportunity in the United States, and thus followed a teaching opportunity overseas to build a relationship with Josai University, for whom we designed over a dozen projects, five of which were built.

Josai University was founded in 1965 by Mikio Mizuta, an economist and Japan's finance minister for much of its postwar growth period. Mizuta is best known for making the modern yen a force in world currency in the mid-1960s by tying it to the dollar at 360 yen, a number that symbolically referenced the cyclical regenerative ethos of Shintoism, to gain the confidence of the Japanese public. Mizuta died in 1976. His daughter, Noriko Mizuta, a renowned scholar of Japanese literature, served as president of Josai International University from 1996 to 2009 and as chancellor of Josai Education University from 1996 until 2016.

Our design and construction partners during this stretch was the Obayashi Corporation, founded in 1892 by Yoshigoro Obayashi, a Kimono merchant from Osaka who repaired temples as a side business. Obayashi is now one of the so-called Big 5 construction companies in Japan, along with Takenaka, Taisei, Kajima, and Shimizu, all of which operate like giant design-build offices. We were fortunate to work with the same core group over the span of fifteen years, including the same construction, design, and engineering teams. While personnel changed, our Japanese collaborators were anchored by Koji Onishi, who went from junior job captain to Obayashi's director of design, all the while remaining the lead singer of a band that exclusively did Van Halen covers.

Whether working with our overseas partners remotely or in person, designing within a building culture with its own specific protocols and language challenges a linear process of simply materializing intention. Indeed, exacerbated by working with associates that are arms of a construction company, exactitude took the form of allowances, goals, and standards to meet. It was therefore crucial to frame exactitude not as an extension of immovable fixity but as a form of continual becoming through adaptive processes to the glitches of cross-cultural collaboration.

Floating Object

In addition to his work as a politician, economist, and educator, Mikio Mizuta amassed an impressive collection of art. We were asked to create a small museum at Josai University in Saitama Prefecture, an hour north Tokyo, that would display the collection on a rotating basis. The centerpiece of the museum is Mizuta's trove of ukiyo-e prints, anchored by nine works by the renowned ukiyo-e artist Sharaku, including one of his most famous, the portrait of the Kabuki actor Ōtani Oniji III. An additional gallery would be dedicated to rotating exhibitions of contemporary crafts. Adjacent to the entrance of the university, the museum also served a more prosaic role as an information and documentation center.

Three Boxes / Two Ramps / Seventeen Cherry Trees

The site for the museum was shaped by both the grid of the campus and the diagonal geometry oriented toward Josai Hill to the west, a compressed area ringed by seventeen cherry trees, none of which could be removed. The required eight thousand square feet necessitated having two floors, while the budget and tight space requirements did not support a freight elevator or a substantial back of the house. We therefore conceived of a building that was grounded in the fixed world of the everyday while floating above it. Not unlike the lotus flower, art would be encased in an object silhouetted against the sky, though clearly connected to the site and the earth.

The museum contains three galleries, one black box encasing the art of the floating world, one meter above grade, one white box for changing exhibits two meters above grade, and a third transparent box, the residual space below the art galleries, encased in glass, where visitors learn about the university and the activities it supports, two meters below grade. This allowed four meters floor to floor from the glass box to the white box. All galleries are served by perimeter ramps for both loading and entry. One meter is the maximum rise, and twelve meters is the maximum run for a ramp in Japan. This set the building's length at approximately twenty-six meters, including landings. The two-meter minimum distance from the core of each cherry tree determined its width. Achieving floating required a process of designing with numbers that were both prosaic and prescribed.

FIGURE 5.2. Mizuta Museum of Art, wiew from the west. Courtesy studioSUMO. Photo: Daici Ano.

120 mm 3-11-2011 140 mm

The outer edges of the ramps were lined by precast panels, giving definition to the volume but having no load-bearing properties. Rather, the galleries hunker down to the site encased in a cast-in-place structure. The white box gallery that cantilevers over the excavated space of the glass box manifests the psychic space of floating above the fixed and the prosaic contained in the glass box. Just a couple of months before construction was to begin, Obayashi, guided by risk management rather than structural exactitude, recommended thin 120-millimeter-diameter columns, mostly to prevent sag and consequent cracking in the concrete. The company described another museum project they had built, by Tomohiko Yamanashi, the design director of Nikken Sekkei, Japan's largest design firm, that also cantilevered and had experienced sagging and cracking. On March 11, 2011 I traveled to the countryside where the museum was located. I entered and ventured to the cantilever, where I first felt a gentle sway and then a violent shaking. Three days later, making my way back to Tokyo following the Great Kanto Earthquake, I no longer had ground to stand on to argue the column proposal. Unfortunately, the recommended diameter had grown to 140 millimeters. Photos were presented to assuage concerns about the columns' girth, showing a short, round man standing next to them who served as both a scale reference and a distraction, making the columns appear thinner, and eschewing the exactitude of structural calculation to instead make a visual case for the negligibility of twenty meters. And, coated with automotive paint, the columns would almost disappear.

52 Panels / 104 Days

The perimeter ramps of the museum were lined by a concrete screen and formed a kind of *engawa* for the galleries, a strip of space between exterior and interior common in traditional Japanese architecture. This space was for both entry and service, and operated as an attenuated threshold between the campus and the galleries, evocative of the trip along the Sumida River from Edo to the floating world of Yoshiwara. The procession was shielded by a second skin, providing shade but not enclosure, with slit-like

FIGURE 5.3. Mizuta Museum of Art, ramped *engawa*. Courtesy studioSUMO.
Photo: Daici Ano.

openings continuing from vertical to horizontal. Rather than risk being cracked by using a cast-in-place process, the walls were conceived of as fifty-two unique L-shaped panels that were seamed together, the largest almost ten meters high, each with an opening at the edge. The panels have two smooth sides with the short end of the L also skewed to the slope of the ramp, necessitating that they be cast on edge. A single mold was made, with one panel being cast every two days (using foam blocks to alter the height and opening location) then left to cure until transported to be assembled together in a two-day period.

The entry facade is framed by two portals, ramping down to the left, and up to the right. A Buddha sculpted by a disgraced former prime minister who took up ceramics in postpolitical life hovers above. Heading down, one arrives at a sunken court, the floating object over the transparent gallery. One enters the museum on axis with the Buddha, the black box to the left of the entry, the white box to the right, and the glass box below, encasing the disappearing columns upon which the volume floats.

Floating Subject

Even before the seventeenth century, when burgeoning Edo challenged the fixity of the social order, the floating subject has been a Japanese fixture, first in its lore, and then in its national narrative of modernization. Indeed, in his "Capsule Declaration" the Japanese architect Kisho Kurokawa cited the kago, which was used to transport nobility, as a cultural precedent for his work.[5] The postwar internationalization of Japan's population, US military occupation, multinational corporations, and, most recently, working-class immigrants has created multiple groups of floating subjects.

Forty-four Rooms / Twenty-four Countries / One Facade

Among the most recent group of floating subjects is the international student. With Japan's declining birth rate, private universities are in dire need of students for financial survival. The international student is increasingly important for universities to maintain their enrollment numbers. Decades ago, Josai University's second campus, Josai International University, not far from Narita Airport in the town of Togane, wisely made alliances with countries of Southeast Asia and the former Soviet Republic.

The university dormitory is relatively rare in Japan, since Japanese students typically stick close to home or rent private apartments.

FIGURE 5.4. Mizuta Museum of Art, north facade. Courtesy studioSUMO.
Photo: Daici Ano.

Given that many of the landlords in this small town were wary of foreign students, the university asked us to design a dormitory, an international house for an international university—an i-house.

The dormitory sits on the far north edge of the campus, and the site's south edge is across the street from the main campus entrance. The north edge is bound by rice fields. The site itself is next to a soccer field and has a retention pond that doubles as an outdoor amphitheater.

To minimize its footprint, the building is a narrow bar at that north edge. A chunk has been taken out to provide an entry court and to frame a view of the rice fields. The court is anchored by a volume containing a collection of public programs, including a small soccer museum, the subject for another essay. The dorm rooms line the north side, facing the fields, and are served by exterior walkways on the south side that are screened by interlaced, off-the-shelf aluminum louvers of varied widths. The walkways themselves widen in areas for students to hang out. The facade blurs the reading of the

FIGURE 5.5. The i-house student dormitory, south facade. Courtesy studioSUMO. Photo: Kawasami Kobayashi Kenji.

dormitory type, one typically marked by repetitive windows on a flat surface. Instead the facade responds to the light over the course of the day, from morning to afternoon. The grain of the facade parallels the approach to the void in the bar from which one enters the building.

Seventy Dollars / Ten Centimeters/ Eight Months

These are three important metrics with little tolerance that guided the design and production of the building.

Seventy dollars refers to the monthly rent, set to accommodate the majority of the students who arrived at the university without much in the way of financial resources. Therefore, living space had to be minimal, and each student was given a storage container in an adjacent structure. The majority of the rooms housed four students, with loft beds and desks underneath. The space was designed with little tolerance for messiness, but the critical condition that arose was the *genkan,* the indispensable sunken space where shoes must be exchanged for slippers. To make the *genkan,* floors are typically built up at least ten centimeters from the subfloor. To make the project economically viable, the university required that the five floors fit within a zoning height limit, which required three-meter floor-to-floor heights. A mechanical soffit dropped the ceiling further, and to meet the 2.2-meter head height while accommodating the ten-centimeter floor rise for the *genkan,* an unorthodox structural solution was required: to eliminate the beams. The walls contain cast-in-place 40-by-120-centimeter "column walls" that are wide enough to provide lateral support. In addition, the floor slabs sandwich three layers: a layer of prefabricated concrete panels, a layer of foam, and a layer of cast-in-place concrete, lightening the slab, eliminating the need for the beam, and accelerating curing time, which allowed the building to be completed in eight months, aligning with the academic calendar. The resulting dorm rooms are very tight, more like a collection of self-contained berths, so spaces of circulation, such as corridors with sliding glass doors that extend space onto the walkways, the walkways themselves, and various outdoor courts, become areas to gather, to breathe, and to float.

FIGURE 5.6. The i-house student dormitory, dormitory *engawa*. Courtesy studio-SUMO. Photo: Kawasami Kobayashi Kenji.

Checking One's Sword

Japanese construction drawing sets are extremely precise, as one would expect, but also extremely concise. A Japanese building is realized with a fraction of the drawings and documents used to outline projects in the United States. This is possible due to heavily prescribed roles and procedures in architect-client and architect-contractor relationships. After a specified period of ideation, there is little space to drift toward possible solutions discovered in the process.

While this linearity is admirable in practice, we were fortunate that the role we played in this process allowed us to circumvent this model of exactitude. For these two projects, and all of our Japanese buildings, studioSUMO was able to occupy a space less grounded or prescribed. Like those who checked their swords before entering Yoshiwara, our role and status were multivalent and at times nebulous. As professors, architects, and foreigners, we took on multiple roles relative to the client, to our associate architects and contractor, and to Japan. Consequently, the numbers, the metricss that guided our process came from multiple directions.

The condition of being simultaneously embedded in the cultural context of the project and untethered from the professional context of our own office resonated with the ideas behind the Mizuta Museum and the condition of the subjects living in the i-house dormitory. We could understand the profundity of a cherry tree, the mystery of Sharaku's legacy, and the loneliness of the international student. These are the spaces that connect the ephemeral with the material and enrich the conception of architecture, spaces through which to travel, through which to float.

NOTES

1 Italo Calvino, "Exactitude," in *Six Memos for the Next Millennium,* trans. Geoffrey Brock (New York: Houghton Mifflin Harcourt, 2016), 68.

2 David Waterhouse, "Hishikawa Moronobu: Tracking Down an Elusive Master," in *Designed for Pleasure: The World of Edo Japan in Prints and Paintings, 1680–1860* (Seattle: University of Washington, 2008), 33.

3 Timon Screech, *Obtaining Images: Art, Production, and Display in Edo Japan* (London: Reaktion Books, 2012), 266.

4 Ibid., 81.

5 Kurokawa Kisho, *Metabolism in Architecture* (Boulder, CO: Westview Press, 1977), 78.

EXACTITUDE AT PLAY

Chapter 6
Stacks

Case Studies in a Construction of Exactitude

LOT-EK: Ada Tolla and Giuseppe Lignano
with Thomas de Monchaux

Because the work of LOT-EK is simple, crude, improvisational, and unoriginal, it speaks directly to a discourse
of exactitude in architecture. To be sure, the work is simple, crude,
improvisational, and unoriginal in a way that also requires it to be
complex, subtle, planned, and unprecedented. One way of narrat-
ing the manifestation of exactitude in architecture is to propose that
the original and specific inspiration of the architect—which generally comes to her with a seemingly incoherent uncertainty and
mutability that can be mistaken for imprecision, and that she then
permutates and iterates in a process that can be mistaken for inde-
cision—is subsequently and conclusively ordered by a sequence of
unoriginal and generic interventions by technicians of engineering
and construction. In theory, these fields are subordinate to architecture but, in practice, architecture is subjected to them. The wild
animal is tamed.

The work of LOT-EK is not like that. We begin with dissections and assemblies of ready-made objects, epitomized by an industrial and infrastructural artifact: the standard ISO shipping container. The initials ISO are significant to a discourse of exactitude, which is neither a self-organizing and self-recognizing phenomenon like those complex homeostatic systems to be found in nature nor, for that reason, an especially self-evident one. The exactitude found or expressed within an object or an apparently closed system is often invented and enforced from without. The exactitude of the shipping container is an artifact of political and industrial power: the International Organization for Standardization, a nongovernmental organization, was founded in 1947, in Geneva, Switzerland—land of diplomatic negotiation and mechanical precision. The ISO has a General Secretariat and a Technical Management Board representing about 160 signatory nations. It inherited the mission of the International Federation of the National Standardizing Associations, a body founded in 1926 with its own precursors dating back to a British convention on screw threads that took place in 1841. In this sense, the shipping container is not a modern marvel, like the Case Study Houses with which it shares so much metalwork and the fact of having been invented in mid-twentieth-century California, but a direct consequence of the mechanical and colonial practices of the illustrious Victorians. In 1968, the ISO finally standardized the shipping container, variations of which had been adapted out of panelized truck beds over the previous twenty years.

As a consequence of this, the shipping container is perpetually a time capsule from 1968. Spatially and materially, it is a box, with two vertically hinged doors at one narrow end, fabricated primarily out of fourteen-gauge weatherized COR-TEN alloy steel corrugated at a two-inch differential orthogonal to its long axis, with exterior dimensions of eight feet wide, eight feet six inches high. About three-quarters of all containers are forty feet long, and the remaining mostly twenty feet long. The container's mass and structure are concentrated in an edge frame, which resolves to heavyweight corner castings at the box's eight vertices. These extend one-eighth of an inch beyond the corrugated steel envelope and feature intersecting tubular channels linking its three outer planes, which enable containers to be stacked and mechanically connected in transit. Typically, they are stacked six or seven containers high, fifteen to twenty containers across, with an on-deck and below-deck capacity of around three thousand containers, holding around one hundred thousand tons of cargo on a typical containerized ship. The typical 150-foot beam of the ship is calibrated to the historical breadth of the Panama Canal. The eight-foot width of the container is calibrated to the historical dimensions of a truck flatbed, which in turn is calibrated to earlier historical widths of roadway lanes of traffic. There are an estimated twenty-five million in-service containers, and a further fifteen million out-of-service containers, all in varying condition and with varying adaptability for reuse. With an average lifespan of twelve years, the nominal obsolescence of standardized shipping containers is not only material or mechanical but also financial. As a matter of carbon, it's appealing to imagine that these durable metal objects have a long operational life cycle of hundreds of round trips. But as a matter of capital, and especially because of imbalances in global trade, it can be far more efficient for containers to be promptly abandoned abroad, in urban-scaled stacks at port cities around the world, without being much reused, reshipped, or ever returned to their common place of origin, China, the leading global exporter of manufactured goods—including 90 percent of all shipping containers.

LOT-EK subjects the shipping container to operations of incision, iteration, combination, and transformation that radically adapt, upcycle, and misuse it in ways that are delicately and intimately informed by the parameters and proprieties of its original intended use. Because of the shipping container's standardized design, built-in exactitude adheres to the object from the beginning, and that inherent precision is co-opted and compounded, not resisted, by our subsequent operations upon it. This built-in exactitude has paradoxical properties, from the quantitative to the qualitative. Quantitatively, it requires the finest fractional calibration, since working primarily in metal allows very little "tolerance"—that problematic word for the skillful operational anticipation of inevitable physical misalignments. But it also requires an interest in basic whole numbers and integral proportions. The box of the container is eight feet by eight feet by forty feet. The mundane ratio of one to five is our golden section. Interestingly, the shipping container is designed to be strongest not in compression but in tension, for the brief perilous moment of craned and suspended motion between deck and port. Qualitatively, the very narrowness and arbitrariness of the container's intended use allows for a breadth and specificity in the manner of its reuse and misuse.

Exactitude can be examined and expressed in several different ways, through three iterations of our recent design research projects: STACKS. In ascending order of permanence and complexity, they are TRIANGLE STACK ONE, TRIANGLE STACK TWO, and DRIVELINES STUDIOS.

These projects are three and one. Sequenced here in a linear and conceptual crescendo, they were nonlinear and nonsequential in time. For the purposes of this essay, LOT-EK has curated and grouped this work to articulate the growth and development of a practice that is visual and material, selective and adaptive—and, despite the generic nature of its unit, highly personal.

The first project, TRIANGLE STACK ONE, is an experiment in restacking and misstacking shipping containers at the Integrated Industries storage facility in Perth Amboy, New Jersey, deploying only the forbearance, embodied intelligence, and gestural skill of vehicle operators. We did this on August 9, 2017, between 11:45 a.m. and 3 p.m. We built two stacks, which existed for a total of seventy-two hours. One of these was Triangle Stack One, which consists of eighteen containers, stacked simply and solidly on three six-level-high sides, to form a triangle volume with a two-foot gap at one corner to allow entry. It took exactly one hour to stack the eighteen containers. We verbally communicated our basic formal intention for the objects to the vehicle operators, supplemented by rudimentary diagrams printed on 8.5 x 11-inch printer paper. We observed the sizable structure taking shape, like watching the sped-up film of a bird building a nest.

The geometrical intention behind TRIANGLE STACK ONE was straightforward: to test a volume at odds with the conventionally orthogonal port stacks of shipping containers, and to develop this volume not as a continuous mass but as an enclosure that alternated solid and void, outlining an unexpected inhabitable interior void. The critical tool was the Empty Container Handler, a forklift

FIGURE 6.1. Triangle Stack One. Courtesy of LOT-EK.

vehicle that can stack up to six containers. It was driven principally by Steve Alo, a veteran foreman of the port. As in a performance, the operation of this vehicle required very specific and proficient skills, highly trained neuromuscular gestures to execute a simple yet precise choreography. No container connectors or clamps were used to physically connect the boxes together. As with a house of cards, the sturdiness and stability of the tall assembly (which rose to almost sixty feet), depended solely on the exact alignment of the containers' stacking points. TRIANGLE STACK ONE was a "rough and ready", "quick and dirty" project. Its making required constant readjustment of its elements and procedures in real-time reciprocity between LOT-EK and Steve Alo. It was reconfiguration as an act of imagination, simultaneously deploying and diverting the existing system that surrounded it. It was a deft action, relying on embodied intelligence and sense memory that spatially translated and transformed a generic box without physically changing it. Quick in the sense of alive, vivid, lively, fleet, nimble, alert, agile—and therefore precise. In this sense, its roughness was a kind of smoothness, and its dirtiness a kind of cleanness—fundamental, essential, exacting in its making though not, in its final form, fully foreseeable.

FIGURE 6.2. Triangle Stack One. Courtesy of LOT-EK.

The second project is TRIANGLE STACK TWO, a 2020 installation of eighteen containers in coastal Brooklyn, New York, developed under the auspices of the Brooklyn Museum, to create a six-story atrium-like public space (utilized as a temporary armature for the display of an artist's mural). This had been planned as a three-month public art installation—extended to eight months due to the global pandemic—onto a temporarily available parcel adjacent to the Domino Sugar Factory, prior to the parcel's development. A structure of only mechanical connections, TRIANGLE STACK TWO was built without on-site welding.

This project required two practices of exactitude. The first of these was the calculation of the volume of water, in plastic tanks within the two bottom-level containers, to provide sufficient counterweight to hurricane wind load in the absence of a physical foundation. This calculation follows the determination that water stored within the lowest tiers of containers—not concrete or stone or more metal—could answer the strict structural code requirements and fixed budgetary limitations. More operationally contingent than the mere volume of water was the amount of time it would take to pump that volume from a nearby municipal hydrant. To fill eighty-eight tanks, 250 gallons each, for a total of 22,000 gallons of generic city water, required forty-four hours, with five people working over ten days.

This practice of exactitude is directly connected to the "quantifiable" pressure, in this case the twenty-pound-per-square-foot code requirement for hurricane-grade uplift wind loads, that would normally require an actual foundation. Our alternative and unconventional solution shifted the idea of a hard and permanent concrete foundation toward its fluid, temporary equivalent, water weight, which was as ephemeral as the installation itself: water flow being collected, measured, and contained, and eventually dispersed as flow again. Because it only temporarily diverts water flow and water storage, this solution is sustainable—and if you seek the poetic it is to be found in the use of the latent storage capacity of the container to house water tanks: the very water that will find its way to the seas on which the container may someday be shipped, dwells for a moment inside its steel walls. The communal task of filling the tanks, shared by five people on the art and design team and not by the contractors, provided a performative test of endurance. A

FIGURE 6.3. Triangle Stack Two. Courtesy of LOT-EK.

repetitive set of operations—in solitude and silence, and in the cold of January's winter—offered a powerful meditative experience of the installation itself through time, through daylight and darkness, in a fast-transforming neighborhood.

The second practice of exactitude in TRIANGLE STACK TWO was the morphing of hardware: the hacking of a component called a "deck connector" into a kind of prosthetic attachment to distort and extend the functionality of the shipping container's corner castings. Typically, containers in transit are held together at their corners by "twist-lock" clamps, designed to allow a quarter-inch displacement or translation between vertically or horizontally adjacent containers. This accommodation of displacement—how far can the system depart from some optimum order and still work—generally goes by two problematic words with opposite connotations: "tolerance" and "play." To tolerate is to have power. To be tolerated is to not have power. To play is to be at liberty—and yet the word in this context describes the limits of freedom.

These standard "twist-locks" are conceived for orthogonal stacking only, precisely to prevent any further possible rotation between top and bottom containers. To achieve further rotation—our required angles between top and bottom containers (55, 55, and 70 degrees respectively)—the standard "twist-lock" is here connected in a nonstandard way to a second standard component, the "deck

FIGURE 6.4. Triangle Stack Two. Courtesy of LOT-EK.

socket" with which containers are attached to ships' decks, and then that assembly is doubled and mirrored, yielding a welded connection assembly that mechanically attaches the two bases together at the desired angle. An install-and-lock sequence was tested, recorded as a tutorial for the installation crew, assembled and welded off-site as an actual artifact, and then closely supervised during on-site assembly. The resulting stack, incorporating forty-five such assemblies, resting on "pins" a few inches taller than a conventional "twist-lock" clamp, elevates the body of the shipping containers 4.5 inches from one another, raising each unit and each level slightly, exposing that single joint as the recognizable point of connection. This precise misuse of the orthogonal default of a preengineered, pretested component yields this 2,800 square-foot, six-story public space, lifting and floating its generic component, the box.

The third project is DRIVELINES STUDIOS, a 2017 apartment building in the emerging neighborhood of Maboneng, Johannesburg, that develops the STACK toward the service systems, structural performance, and enclosure that are required by permanent buildings. DRIVELINES is a seventy-five-thousand-square-foot, seven-story complex of about one hundred mostly studio apartments. It responds to the postapartheid generation's intention to repopulate the city's downtown through new models of urban living. Two narrow bar buildings, constituted by sixty-eight and seventy-two shipping containers arranged longitudinally at two or three containers' width, form an intimate V-shaped courtyard, overlooked by open-air semiprivate corridor balconies converging at a circulation core. The third leg of the triangle is here left open to views of the skyline of the central business district of Johannesburg. The shipping containers, sourced at City Deep, Johannesburg's dry shipping container port situated less than one mile away from the site, were old and worn. All exactly blue. None exactly blue. Not enough blue containers were available, so the second large batch was green. Exactitude, as Italo Calvino ventures in his famous essay on the subject, can be approached along seemingly opposite trajectories: through an "abstract rational" mental scheme of connecting lines of thought, or through the "fine dust" of accumulated description, of seemingly too many words. Our work deepens this paradox: on the one hand, the container is a preconceived constant that, while concrete and not abstract, nevertheless rationalizes its

FIGURE 6.5. Drivelines Studios. Photo: Dave Southwood.

contents and constructs, and engages geometry through cuts and stacks—our own "abstract rational"; on the other hand, the container, as we find it, is always too much and too late: a ubiquitously and continuously accumulating leftover—our own "fine dust" of, seemingly, too many boxes.

The most significant practice of exactitude at DRIVELINES is in the on-site fabrication of the structure. In the design discourse of the developed West and Global North, there seems to be a fondness for the idea of prefabrication, especially when it comes to housing: the idea that homes can—and so should—be premade off-site, with all the purported consumer economy and apparent manufacturing efficiency of the refrigerators and automobiles with which they will later be filled. We have explored the myths and realities of prefabrication in our own work, most recently in our c-Home series of freestanding houses, the first of which was recently constructed near the container ports of New Jersey and sited 150 miles away in upstate New York's Hudson Valley. But at Maboneng, the opposite was true. Prefabricated components must generally be designed to be independently structurally integral, prior to their incorporation into a collective structure—like the container, they must work in multiples of one as well as of thousands. But we realized that by stacking the containers on-site, and only subsequently incising and reinforcing them, we could use half the reinforcing steel that would otherwise be required. Welded together, and reinforced by leftovers from the window cutouts, the facing channels of adjacent corrugated container surfaces become the functional equivalent of steel columns—which would otherwise have had to redouble this detail in numbers, as well as be separately made and applied—both constituted by and supporting the whole. Local economies of labor and material—which, to be sure, are not universal—made this approach both necessary and possible. For a discourse of exactitude, we emphasize the downstreaming of problem solving. We did not get ahead of the problem, we got behind the labor expertise that we discovered on-site—a simple example of which was a degree of precision in manual steel-craft that we might have thought achievable only with mechanized or automated systems. Learning from DRIVELINES and our stack projects more generally, we have begun to postrationalize much of our body of work, with its successive on- and off-site modifications of ready-made source objects, as a practice of postfabrication.

At DRIVELINES, the structural thinking that began with these columns extends to a system of cuts that open the container to the elements and to daylight. Repeated and mirrored, front and rear, a diagonal line allows the reinforcement around the incised edge to double as cross-bracing against shear. The design strategy of both building up and opening up the structure extends to the slenderness of the two building wings, allowing cross-ventilation and passive cooling. It also opens up an abundance of commons along balconies and other circulation spaces. As a result, spaces that would otherwise be unused become unpredictable, serendipitous, and fortuitous areas of social encounter in this postapartheid urban community among neighbors who now call themselves "driveliners." The building's social intention and agenda are aligned with the emerging urban community of its surrounding neighborhood, taking an active role in the revitalization, reactivation, and reimagining of the city's

FIGURE 6.6. Drivelines Studios. Photo: Dave Southwood.

downtown. Although constructed in ways that required predictability and reproducibility, DRIVELINES subsequently becomes an armature and catalyst for social improvisation and invention.

A much-quoted passage from Calvino's essay "Exactitude,"
in the standard 1988 English edition (written as one of Calvino's
undelivered 1985 Norton Lectures and translated by Patrick Creagh
for Harvard University Press), states, "The word connects the visible trace with the invisible thing, the absent thing, the thing that is
desired or feared, like a frail emergency bridge flung over an abyss."
As Italians, and more importantly as Neapolitans, we at LOT-EK
propose a more exact translation. The meaning of the text's original Italian word *vuoto* is not "abyss" but "void": a neutral, mundane, simple, clear word that connotes lightness and openness,
or mere absence, as much as the heaviness and gravity of a long
fall. The word "emergency" is absent from the original Italian; the
expression used by Calvino is *ponte di fortuna,* a vernacular idiom

suggesting a fortunate bridge, a fortuitous bridge, a serendipitous bridge—a bridge if not in preconceived or customary form, then in effect, in fact, by use through imaginative action. A better translation from that Italian vernacular would point to the meaning of "makeshift" or "make-do" in English: in a happy confluence of happenstance and desire, we improvise and transform what we have into what we need. There is no emergency. Or the emergency is continuous and ubiquitous. We live on that bridge.

In his essay, Calvino tackles limits and measures. He addresses how anything determined and precise inherently opens the way to all that is left out, to all of its possible variations. In our practice, we also attend to limits and their transcendence, to the exhaustion of all the possible variations and iterations, and to details. The three TRIANGLE STACKS presented here are a sample from an ongoing obsession: the systematic testing of STACKS, a long-term project that explores all the generic variations of a six-level-high stack of containers to generate volume and space. With this and related projects of ours, we seek to bridge a false divide between the conceptual and the instrumental, the theoretical and the practical. Work done and undone generates an index or a manual for a landscape of possibilities that our past and future projects inhabit and construct.

The sentence in Calvino's essay following the word "abyss" is, in our own translation from the Italian: "For this reason the proper use of language, to me, is one of approaching things (present or absent) with discretion and attention and care, and with respect for what things (present or absent) communicate without words." Or, in the original: "Per questo il giusto uso del linguaggio per me è quello che permette di avvicinarsi alle cose (presenti o assenti) con discrezione e attenzione e cautela, col rispetto di ciò che le cose (presenti o assenti) comunicano senza parole." We respect and relate to Calvino's use of the word "thing," the most generic of words, but also the most inclusive and adaptive. A word that says and does almost nothing, and that can almost say and do it all. Just like our thing, our box.

Chapter 7

Machine Consequences

Alicia Imperiale

Material behaviors are always studied in architecture—
for instance, the "aliveness" of concrete is tested in on-
site slump tests of concrete mix during construction. The behaviors of matter—what Jane Bennett calls "vibrant matter"[1] or Gilbert
Simondon described as "individuations"[2]—offer different answers
to architect Louis I. Kahn's question "What does the brick want
to be?" that assumes an already technologically mediated form of
matter. These alternative modes question the molecular makeup of
materials, their kinetic properties and behaviors, and posit the artist as a translator, a trans-maker, revealing scalar changes in matter
and the question of exactitude.

Today, computer numerical control (CNC) machines, which
have been developed to be precise to multiple decimal places,
mill titanium jet engine turbines and automobile engine parts. 3D
printers used in fabricating scientific and medical equipment or in
the precise assembly of manufactured parts through robotic arms

are examples of machines that are creatively misused by artists and designers; this challenges the imperative of dimensional exactitude so critical in industrial manufacturing. As artists and designers experiment with digital output machines, they become a translational device from code to matter. The artist's hand pushes against the exact dimensional tolerances these machines afford, embracing the messiness of material and matter itself. The designer's handiwork appears in the interplay of machine and material, in turn allowing the inconsistencies in matter to become visible.

Contemporary architects and artists have been experimenting with unconventional assemblages of 3D printers, hacking machines with unusual and unexpected materials. Rael San Fratello architects used the residue of grapes pressed to make wine that was then mixed with epoxy to 3D print organic building blocks; Terreform One proposed 3D printing pig cells to form what they called a "victimless shelter." Existing machines are rethought to create large-scale structures: a robotic arm was reconfigured by the Joris Laarman lab to move along a gantry system to print a steel bridge over a canal in Amsterdam. In *Cement Room,* his installation at the Barbara Gladstone Gallery, artist Anish Kapoor used a 3D printer to extrude concrete. Rather than allowing each layer of concrete to harden before another was added, the weight of the viscous matter of the concrete bulged, broke, and oozed, showing the dynamic effect of gravity on the material. Instead of attempting to produce a successful 3D print, Kapoor reveled in the playful act of subverting the intended precision of the machine. These are just some of the human-animal-mineral experiments seen in today's architectural and artistic practices. These examples are all digital output devices, which means that the object is designed with CAD software and then the digital file is exported to STL code, which translates the digital model into directions for the machine to create the 3D-printed or CNC-milled object. So it is in this sense that the expression "machine consequences" encompasses the tension between a machine that is calibrated to be precise and exact in manufacturing processes and the creative play of the artist who finds a different kind of value in the imprecise and the inexact.[3] In this spirit, I will focus on an avant-garde artist active in the 1960s and 1970s who did not work a digital output machine but with another machine, the Xerox photocopier.

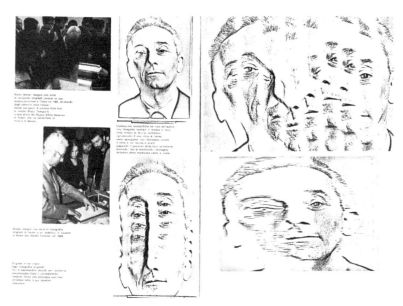

FIGURE 7.1. Bruno Munari making a series of "xerox originals" in public in Tokyo in 1965 and with students in Rome in 1969. Top left is a xerox of a photograph of Munari and the resulting xerox experiments of his self-portrait. In Bruno Munari, *Xerografia: Documentazione sull'uso creative delle macchine Rank Xerox*, 1970, unpaginated. https://www.munart.org/doc/bruno-munari-xerografia-1970-rank-xerox.pdf.

The Italian artist Bruno Munari (1907–1998) experimented with a Xerox machine in making what he called *Xerografia originali*, or "original xeroxes." Although Munari did not work at an architectural scale, he presented a methodology as well as a political stance regarding artistic creation that is still relevant today. He observed that in the field of "aesthetic research," as he called it, "visual operators" have long been attracted to technological innovation and new instruments. He presciently wrote that the tools, or machines, that were first invented to reduce human labor and to increase productivity have been historically repurposed by artists to explore and experiment in the field of aesthetic creativity.[4]

The rise of bureaucracy and globalization propelled numerous inventions throughout the second half of the twentieth century. In 1959, the exact reproduction of documents in seconds became a reality with the successful production on an industrial scale of the

Xerox 914 machine. The Xerox machine made it possible to create high-speed and virtually infinite exact copies. While xeroxing revolutionized the business world, the expanded possibilities of reproduction were felt far beyond the walls of commerce.[5] Much as we have seen 3D printers, CNC mills, and robotic arms make their way into schools of architecture over the past twenty years, universities and other cultural institutions leased the Xerox 914. Before long, one could register the impact of this technology—its appropriation and use in experimental artistic practices.

American artist Mel Bochner's 1966 *Working Drawings and Other Visible Things on Paper Not Necessarily Meant to Be Viewed as Art* set a precedent for presenting Xerox copies within a gallery setting. Bochner, at the time an instructor in art history at the School of Visual Arts in New York City, was asked to curate an exhibit in the school's gallery space. The exhibit ran on an extremely tight budget, and there were no funds for framing the works. Instead, he chose to show the "working drawings," such as receipts, sketches, correspondence, and the like, rather than the final products, of artists such as Donald Judd, Eva Hesse, Dan Graham, and Sol LeWitt. Bochner had unlimited access to a Xerox machine (presumably the Xerox 914). As he copied the original materials, which varied in size, color, and media, he realized that the uniform copies that emerged could be assembled into a book. Then Bochner, within the bare walls of the white gallery space, exhibited four identical three-ring binders, set on white cube pedestals in the center of the space. In this exhibit, the use of a Xerox machine as tool and the Xerox copy as medium became a material foil for larger conceptual discussions regarding seriality that Bochner was exploring.[6] Seriality investigated through the reproduction and repetition of an image or element is a methodological approach that was exhaustively explored in the late 1950s and throughout the 1960s. Rotation, scaling, and permutation were some of the techniques employed in order to remove the hand of the artist as author and to speak to the systemization of form creation.

In Italy, Bruno Munari also began his work with a Xerox machine in the early 1960s. Munari's use of the Xerox machine as an instrument for making art supported the contention that technological reproduction had merged with the intellectual concerns of seriality in art production. The fusion of technique and idea was absorbed into art making, product design, and the architectural prefabrication concepts and processes that had currency in Italy during the 1960s.[7]

In a key move, Munari looked at both the capabilities and fidelity of the photocopied image, on the one hand, and the possibilities latent in the degradation of an image produced by making copies of copies. His series, titled *Sparizione dell'immagine* (The Disappearing Image) and the *Distorted Portrait Xerox 4000*, are documented in the catalogue *Xerografia: Documentatione sull'uso creative delle macchine Rank Xerox* (Xerography: Documentation of the Creative Use of the Rank Xerox Machine), published in 1972.[8]

Munari also created a beautiful series of repetitively patterned Xerox works titled *Xerografia originale*. These images speak to his continued engagement with the Xerox machine in making original works of art. In its intended purpose, the machine would produce an exact facsimile of the original, and in order to create a good copy

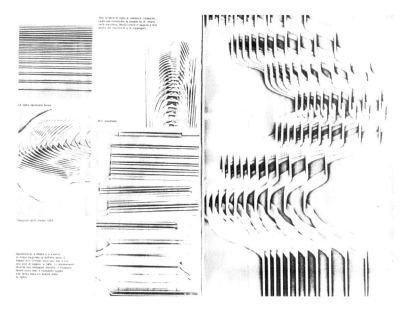

FIGURE 7.2. Munari drew and then xeroxed a series of graduated lines (seen in the upper left) and used this simple drawing to experiment and catalog the effect of different movements. The image on the far right is reproduced in the Venice Biennial catalog and was produced by moving the original drawing from right to left on a diagonal as the light passed below the glass scanning surface. In Bruno Munari, *Xerografia: Documentazione sull'uso creative delle macchine Rank Xerox,* Milan: Rank Xerox, S.p.A.,1970, unpaginated, https://www.munart.org/doc/bruno-munari-xerografia -1970-rank-xerox.pdf.

one would have to place the original document in a fixed position on the glass scanning surface. Instead, Munari experimented with what he described as "embedding time" in the Xerox copy. Each of his *Xerografie originale* is a unique record of a dynamic process, an original work of art. In his performance, Munari created Xerox originals from different materials, such as photographs, other images, nonfigurative perforated plastic sheets, meshes, organic materials, transparent plastics, and paper of varying colors and degrees of thickness and transparency. Using various models of photocopiers, he adjusted and played with the toner, and the reduction and enlargement settings, thus setting the mechanical options of the machines as productive variables in the production of the image. In one approach, he placed dimensional materials on the glass surface of the copier and dragged the original across while the light scanned from left to right below the surface: these unique actions were recorded on the resulting print. In the example shown in the exhibition catalogue, white bands in a regular sinusoidal pattern that break up the original image reveal a surprising result that embeds the original, the moving light, and Munari's actions. Other *Xerografie originale* recorded the complete degradation of an image to a pattern of particles. In each of these images, however, Munari was drawn to the repetition of identical elements, revealing patterns in the copy such as bands, concentric geometry, and series.[9]

For a theoretical framework, one may refer to Johan Huizinga's *Homo Ludens: A Study of the Play Element in Culture* as an enactment of the inexact. It is interesting to think about play as "a free activity standing quite consciously outside 'ordinary' life, as being 'not serious,' but at the same time absorbing the player intensely and utterly."[10] In his study *Man, Play, and Games,* Roger Caillois pushed against some of the more rule-bound definitions of play in Huizinga's work, seeing play as "an occasion of pure waste: waste of time, energy, ingenuity, skill, and often of money."[11] Play is also an essential aspect of human social interaction. Caillois also made the important point that play is uncertain, and while there are rules to be followed to allow all players equal opportunity, the end result is not predetermined. He discussed different kinds of games, such as competition, simulation, vertigo, and chance. It is the aspect of chance that I will explore in my discussion of Munari's work with the Xerox machine: embracing chance is a liberating act that has the potential to be

FIGURE 7.3. Bruno Munari and a collective of artists at the 35th Venice Biennale *in 1970*. In Umbro Apollonio, Luciano Caramel, Dietrich Mahlow, eds., Ricerca e Progettazione: Proposte per una esposizione sperimentale, *35th Biennale Internazionale d'Arte di Venezia* (Venice: Ente Autonomo "La Biennale di Venezia," 1970), 128.

political. This aspect of Munari's work is an important lens to bring to contemporary experimentation with output machines.[12]

At the 35th Venice Biennale in 1970, Bruno Munari and a collective of twenty-six like-minded artists were invited to participate in a "Research Laboratory." They produced work using various contemporary machines, such as the silk-screen press, Plexiglas cutters, polystyrene cutters, lithographic stones and press, a vacuum table, and, notably, a Rank Xerox RX 720 machine.[13] The creative potential of *homo ludens* was on full view at the exhibit.

The processes and materials speak of the time: the boom in plastics and the availability of polystyrene and Plexiglas were essential to Andy Warhol's silk screen prints and Roy Lichtenstein's paintings based on comic book cells. These works were included in the 32nd Venice Biennale of 1964, which introduced American pop art to Italy. Lichtenstein referred to American pop art not as American painting but as "industrial painting."[14] The transatlantic movement of these ideas is evident in the technological tools and new materials processed in the "Research Laboratory," such as the silk-screen press, or the airbrush ink that updated the classical art of lithography. Other artists did wet-process photography using large-scale enlargers and printing on the unconventional substrate of canvas. Even the printing press elevated domestic objects and decentered their original meaning. Ernesto Tatafiore's *Rilievo su carta* used the printing press to create a relief of various objects in the pressed paper.

In the context of the political turmoil of the late 1960s, the participants in the "Research Laboratory" saw themselves as "visual operators" who chose to work in sight of the public so as to challenge the institutional status of art exhibitions and the subservience of art objects to the logic of capitalism. While these artists were hosted by the institution of the Venice Biennale, they took a critical stance toward it as they questioned the value of the work of art. In producing work in situ in the gallery, they saw art making as a process, a means, and not just an end, embracing operations that brought into play elements of chance and surprise.

FIGURE 7.4. A group of schoolchildren look down on artist Fabrizio Plessi working on a silk-screen press. From Umbro Apollonio, Luciano Caramel, Dietrich Mahlow, eds., *Ricerca e Progettazione: Proposte per una esposizione sperimentale,* 35th Biennale Internazionale d'Arte di Venezia (Venice: Ente Autonomo "La Biennale di Venezia," 1970), 128.

The artists worked in a series of lowered spaces in full view of the public, who could look down on them. While the onlookers' elevated point of view allowed them to have a better understanding of how the artists worked, the separation between audience and artist was still in place. This gap was bridged through the Xerox machine. With a Rank Xerox machine in place, and reams of A4 paper, Munari used the machine during the exhibition, but, more importantly, visitors to the exhibition were invited to use the Xerox machine to produce their own original work of art. As a consequence, the role of "visual operator" extended to the viewers.[15] This is just as significant as the fact that the artists were no longer working alone in their studios but in public, process was valued more than the final artwork. Visitors to the exhibition could understand the possible variations that working with the machines invited by playing with a machine themselves.

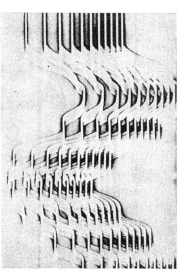

ERNESTO TATAFIORE

Militari di carta, 1970.
Rilievo su carta, cm. 70x100.

XEROGRAFIA

eseguita con una macchina Rank Xerox
da Bruno Munari, cm. 29x21.

FIGURE 7.5. Ernesto Tatafiore, *Rilievo su carta*, 1970 and *Xerografia*, executed on a Rank Xerox machine by Bruno Munari in Umbro Apollonio, Luciano Caramel, Dietrich Mahlow, eds., *Ricerca e Progettazione: Proposte per una esposizione sperimentale*, 35th Biennale Internazionale d'Arte di Venezia (Venice: Ente Autonomo "La Biennale di Venezia," 131.

In the catalogue for the exhibition, Munari did not credit himself as the author of the work: he wrote that the piece, titled *Xerografia,* was "executed" by Bruno Munari. It is the removal of the artist as author and the artist's new status as a "visual operator" that I find most intriguing about Munari's work. He was instrumental in destabilizing the status of the artwork in a gallery or museum setting. A large number of different series of his Xerox art is documented in the publication *Xerografia: Documentazione sull'uso creative delle macchine Rank Xerox.*[16] Each xerox reveals a set of steps or rules for action. These are deliberate acts, revealing the interaction of person and machine. Rotation, scaling, and permutation are some of the techniques Munari employed to remove the hand of the artist as author and to speak to the systemization of form creation. The conceptual use of seriality and permutation connects Munari's work with Mel Bochner's theoretical writing. As Bochner argued, "Serial or systematic thinking has generally been considered the antithesis of artistic thinking. Systems are characterized by regularity, thoroughness, and repetition in execution. They are methodical. It is their consistency and the continuity of application that characterizes them. Individual parts of a system are not in themselves important but are relevant only in how they are used in the enclosed logic of the whole series."[17] By speaking of series and ordered structures, I intentionally want us to think about another kind of exactitude, one that is not precise in dimensional tolerances in fabrication or in the zeros and ones of computation but a set of relations in serial repetition and the adherence to a "progressional procedure," as Bochner called it, that produces variation and change.

The serial removes totality; it is a method, a set of rules that engage chance.[18] The serial is rule-based and, like language, points to an infinite number of possibilities. Working in series opens up the possibility of indeterminacy, as seen in the scientific writings on information theory in *A Mathematical Theory of Communication* by Warren Weaver and Claude E. Shannon.[19] Critics such as Umberto Eco, Abraham A. Moles, Max Bense, Gillo Dorfles, and Lara Vinca Masini have also analyzed seriality in relation to art. Working in series is open and doesn't predict a particular outcome. Working in series invites novel combinations, yet is also rule-based, and in that sense, as in a game, or in play, there are rules. Rules could be established in the spirit of Huizinga and Caillois, as a liberating action, that would go beyond personal creativity and into a more socially related act. The use of chance is governed by combinatorial logic, algorithms, permutation, and iteration—all with an operative rigor.[20] Artists, working with games of chance to question the role of the artist in the production of the final art object, destabilize the precise categorizations of artist, artwork, and artistic environment.

In his 1962 book *Simbolo, comunicazione, consumo*, the Italian critic and philosopher Gillo Dorfles extended the discussion of series and rule-based operations to product design and architecture.[21] Dorfles decoupled "sign" from "design" (*segno* from *disegno*) and in doing so worked against a holistic view of architecture. Not unlike what happens in information theory, a message, or in this case a building, could be broken down into the smallest possible element (such as the word in information theory), and the series of elements could then be reassembled into a unique finished product. Prefabricated building components could be repeated in creating a new assembly, and repetition could then be nuanced with an underlying series of changes. Rather than producing exact replicas, by varying combinations of building components, one could always produce an original composition, much in the same way that Munari created *Xerografie originale*. Dorfles called this the "phenomenon of the custom made."[22] The implications of these processes for design in Dorfles's time are still relevant given the contemporary use of computer-numerically-controlled manufacturing: Dorfles spoke directly about the fusion of "serial production" with the "custom-made," creating the paradoxical neologism "mass-customization" that has been a topic of significant discussion in digital architecture and fabrication.

Another example is found in artist Enzo Mari's work. In the essay "Analogy between Serial Structures and Natural Phenomena and the Programming of Perceptive Phenomena," Mari bridged the concepts of the serial process with the natural permutation of forms. He posited a kind of organicism deeply rooted in the organization of serial elements, whether they be animal, vegetable, or mineral; visible to the human eye or seen only with the aid of a telescope or a microscope; or understood only on a theoretical level in physics or through mathematical formulae. As Mari explained, "All

natural phenomena of any order . . . are always organized according
to series of numerous similar particles that are concretized in modular structures that vary according to very simple sets of rules [fol-
lowed] to form a new modular ensemble."[23] The simple rules that
govern the variation of pattern in his different works connect his
approach to natural rules of growth and form. In the early 1960s,
Mari made a series of sculptural works in which he studied the
variation of a simple module and followed a set of instructions for
their displacement and variation within a given frame. The outer
frame defined the finite space within which the permutation of the
individual module would occur.

Consistent with these operational processes, an idea that was
investigated at a small scale was also explored at an entirely different scale. In 1965, Enzo Mari developed this permutational process
in collaboration with architect Bruno Morassutti. The project was
documented by Lara Vinca Masini in her essay "Arte programmata
e prefabbricazione."[24]

Vinca Masini discussed the Mari and Morassutti project as a
synthesis of different disciplines, an "organic" project fusing art,
science, and technology. She believed that the project represented
a way to reposition the importance of artistic language in a culture
that was becoming increasingly deaf to art as it became increasingly technologically driven. The collaboration between an architect and an artist invested prefabrication with a full range of critical concepts that were used to describe serial art and the Italian
programmed art movement.[25] At the architectural scale, the project
played on the thematic variations of architectural spaces, the rap-
port of different colors in materials, and variations in volumes, as
well as the kinetic aspect of the sliding volumes. This proposal for
programmed prefabrication was intended to act against the monot-
onous regularity that prefabrication usually offers, by planning the
changes through numerically modified modular sequences. While
this project offered a clear example how a serial or rule-based
approach can engage with playful operations to create original
works, it did not involve the future occupant in the design, a point
that Gillo Dorfles discussed in his essay "'Comunicazione' e 'Consumo' nell'arte d'oggi," which introduced two key terms, "communication" and "consumption." Speaking about "works of art" rather
than "painting" or "sculpture," Dorfles argued that the "work of art"

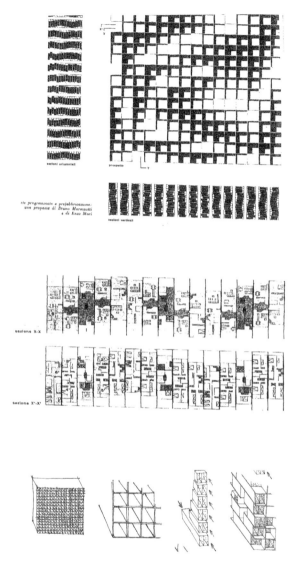

FIGURE 7.6. The diagram at the top provides the instructions for the "programmed development" of the apartment elements that are designed to fit into an overall gridded, reinforced concrete structure. The instructions are to start in the upper left and count to six (each number representing an interval of how much the block is to be recessed from the front face of the frame) and then count back to one and begin again. The other images are horizontal and vertical sections, and a rudimentary set of furnished floor plans that give the project scale. Bruno Morassutti and Enzo Mari, a programmed prefabricated housing proposal in Lara Vinca Masini, "Arte Programmata e Prefabbricazione," in *Domus* 428 (July 1965): 13–15.

speaks a new language that "permits a particular osmosis of the artistic event between the creator and the public. Such osmosis is typical of this kind of work; its social aspect provides a clear connection with programmed art and prefabricated architecture.[26]

In his 1968 essay "Experimental Aesthetic in the New Consumer Society," Abraham A. Moles, a pioneer in the fields of information science and communication studies, spoke about the interrelationship between aesthetics and politics. His writings paralleled and inspired artistic movements; he played an important role in the evolution of the artwork through his book *Théorie de l'information et perception esthétique* (Information Theory and Aesthetic Perception), published in 1958. Moles believed that both the viewer of the work and the artwork as object and process were necessary for the completion of the work itself. Moles reaffirmed the social role of the artwork (and artist) and what he termed "experimental aesthetics." As he pointed out, "Experimental aesthetics is becoming a discipline of considerable social importance. The importance of a social fact is determined by its 'mass effect,' which is calculated, more or less, from the number of people influenced by it, weighted by the degree of influence they each experience. It seems likely that the applications of experimental aesthetics must soon give it a considerable 'mass effect' in society."[27]

Drawing from Walter Benjamin's essay "The Work of Art in the Age of Mechanical Reproduction," Moles predicted that a work of art would reach a larger audience through the proliferation and dissemination made possible by technological innovation and duplication.[28] Moles proposed a new kind of creation that reflected the "dynamism of a culture": "There are no artworks anymore; there are artistic situations and those situations divide, of their own accord, into clearly distinct categories: the category of *creation* and the category of *consumption*."[29] Moles also redefined the artist as aesthetician: "The artist was, in the past, unique and personal; he is now a *metteur en œuvre*, a 'programmer of the beautiful.' He exploits for his own ends the work of the aesthetician who experiments on the perception of originality, on semantic or aesthetic pleasure, and their combination."[30]

To return to the *Xerografie originale* project by Bruno Munari, the "programmer of the beautiful" is now no longer a role that falls solely to the artist. By inviting the public at the 35th Venice

Biennale to use the Xerox machine to make original works of art, Munari embraced the idea that art could be open to all. In the act of play, a technological tool designed to make exact facsimiles of an original document was subverted to allow for infinite variation and experimentation, ultimately inviting everyone to be an artist and produce a work of aesthetic value.

NOTES

1 Jane Bennett, *Vibrant Matter: A Political Ecology of Things* (Durham, NC: Duke University Press, 2010).

2 Gilbert Simondon, "L'individu et sa genèse, forme et matière," in *L'Individuation à la lumière des notions de forme et d'information* (Paris: Presses Universitaires de France, 1964), 66–69.

3 This essay, which focuses on the Xerox machine in artistic practices, is part of a larger book project titled *Machine Consequences: Origins of Output* in which I examine digital output machines such as the laser cutter, CNC mill, 3D printer, and robotic arm, all of which are devices used to manufacture a product that is designed on a computer. I view the Xerox machine as a transitional device, and in studying the work of Bruno Munari ask questions about the social and political implication of his work to guide discussions about contemporary art.

4 Bruno Munari, "Arte e Tecnologia," in *Arte e Xerografia* (Milan: Rank Xerox, S.p.A., 1972), unpaginated.

5 David Owen, *Copies in Seconds: How a Lone Inventor and an Unknown Company Created the Biggest Communication Breakthrough since Gutenberg; Chester Carlson and the Birth of the Xerox Machine* (New York: Simon & Schuster, 2004). See also the collections at the Computer History Museum, https://www.computerhistory.org/collections/, and the Xerox Historical Archives, Webster Campus, near Rochester, NY.

6 James Meyer, "The Second Degree: Working Drawings and Other Visible Things on Paper Not Necessarily Meant to Be Viewed as Art," in *Mel Bochner: Thought Made Visible, 1966–1973* (New Haven, CT: Yale University Art Gallery, 1996), 102. See also Johanna Burton, *Mel Bochner: Language, 1966–2006* (Chicago, IL: Art Institute of Chicago, 2007), 126.

7 Some of Munari's earliest experiments with the Xerox machine took place in 1963–64. These works are held in the Archivio CSAC Università di Parma and in the Fondazione Vodoz-Danese, Milano. The earliest mention of his work with the Xerox was in *Domus* 459 (February 1968), https://www.munart.org/index.php?p=20.

8 Bruno Munari, *Xerografia: Documentazione sull'uso creative delle macchine Rank Xerox*, (Milan: Rank Xerox, S.p.A., 1970).

9 In his *Xerografia Originale* (1963), "Milano propongono originali in serie," he discussed the provocation of originals in series.

10 Johan Huizinga, *Homo Ludens: A Study of the Play Element in Culture* (London: Routledge & Kegan Paul, 1938), 13.

11 Roger Caillois, *Man, Play, and Games* (Champaign: University of Illinois Press, 2001, 1958), 12. His concept of *alea*, or chance, "reveals the favor of destiny"; see 17–19.

12 In my presentation for the conference, I referred to contemporary practices in a more direct way, showing the work of Anish Kapoor, Mitchell Joachim, Neri Oxman, Jenny Sabin, and others.

13 *Ricerca e progettazione: Proposte per una esposizione sperimentale*, 35th Biennale Internazionale d'Arte di Venezia (Venice: Ente Autonomo "La Biennale di Venezia," 1970). In English, *Research and Design: Proposals for an Experimental Exhibit*, 35th Venice Biennale of 1970.

14 John Coplans, *Roy Lichtenstein* (New York: Praeger, 1972), 55.

15 G. Franco Tramontin, *Ricerca e Progettazione: Proposte per una esposizione sperimentale*, 35th Biennale Internazionale d'Arte di Venezia (Venice: Ente Autonomo "La Biennale di Venezia," 1970), 121. Gianni Bertini, "Perché un laboratorio di ricerca," in *Ricerca e Progettazione: Proposte per una esposizione sperimentale*, 35th Biennale Internazionale d'Arte di Venezia (Venice: Ente Autonomo "La Biennale di Venezia," 1970), 135.

16 Munari began working with a Xerox 914 machine in 1963 and continued throughout his career. His images were always originals, *xerografie originale,* and would range from figurative to abstract as he would move the original across the glass scanning surface of the xerox for the duration of the scan In this publication, he also gives instructions on the many ways to subvert the commercial machine's function to create original artworks and images.

17 Mel Bochner, "Serial Art/Systems: Solipsism," *Arts Magazine* (Summer 1967): 39–43.

18 On the idea of chance, or *caso*, as instrumental in making art, see Umberto Eco, "The Form of Disorder," in *Gianni Colombo*, ed. Marcella Beccaria (Milano: Skira, 2009), 210–13. Originally published in Umberto Eco, "La forma del disordine," in *Almanacco letterario Bompiani: Le Applicazioni dei calcolatori elettronici alle scienze morali e alla letteratura* (Milano: Bompiani & C., 1961), 175–88.

19 Claude E. Shannon and Warren Weaver, *A Mathematical Theory of Communication* (Chicago, IL: University of Illinois Press, 1949).

20 The underlying question in much of programmed art is that it was meant to subvert the capitalist structure by actively involving the viewer in the performance of the work, diminishing the role of the artist in the production of art, and intentionally undermining the capacity of a work of art to be reduced to a consumer object. It is probably safe to say that these goals were not attained as the works were collected, exhibited, and so on, and thus complicit with the capitalist project. However, it is still very important to discuss the work within the context of the moment, and the opti-

mism inherent in the success of opposition, a point that is as important today as it was more than fifty years ago.

21 Gillo Dorfles, *Simbolo, comunicazione, consumo* (Torino, Italy: Giulio Einaudi editore, 1962), 205.

22 Ibid.

23 Enzo Mari, *Funzione della ricerca estetica/The Function of Esthetic Research* (Milan, Italy: Edizioni di Comunità, 1970), 38–39.

24 Lara-Vinca Masini, "Arte Programmata e Prefabbricazione," in *Domus* 428 (July 1965): 13–15.

25 The exhibit was *Arte programmata: Arte cinetica, opere moltiplicate, opera aperta* (Programmed art: Kinetic art, multiples, open work) (Milan, Italy: Officina d'arte grafica A. Lucini, 1962). *Arte Programmata* (for short) is the title of an exhibition and catalogue sponsored by the Olivetti Foundation at its showroom in Milan in March 1962. The exhibit was conceived and organized by Bruno Munari, with the intellectual rigor of the accompanying text by Umberto Eco. In his essay, Eco discussed the expressive possibility of the computer. He speaks of a new kind of artist, who would work not with harmonious, Pythagorean sequences, but who understands the fecundity of change and disorder (*caso e del disordine*); such an artist would utilize, but not bow toward, scientific methods by looking toward statistics and putting a more casual spin on the processes of creation, and would look for the poetic in the geometric and discover the "possibility of the formal in the informal (*scoprendo le possibilità formali dell'informe*), that is, how to give a form, a new form, to that which was always considered a pure state of disorder. It was Eco's call to reuse the logic of seriality, to break it open and play with new rules.

26 Gillo Dorfles, "'Comunicazione' e 'Consumo' nell'arte d'oggi," in *Azimuth* 1 (1959), inside front cover.

27 Abraham A. Moles, "Experimental Aesthetics in the New Consumer Society," in *A Little-Known Story about a Movement, a Magazine, and the Computer's Arrival in Art: New Tendencies and Bit International, 1961–1973*, ed. Margit Rosen (Karlsruhe, Germany: ZMK, 2011), 300.

28 Walter Benjamin, "The Work of Art in the Age of Its Technological Reproducibility: Second Version," in Walter Benjamin, *The Work of Art in the Age of Its Technological Reproducibility and Other Writings on Media*, ed. Michael W. Jennings, Brigid Doherty, and Thomas Y. Levin, trans. Edmund Jephcott, Rodney Livingstone, Howard Eiland, et al. (Cambridge, MA: The Belknap Press of Harvard University Press, 2008), 20.

29 Moles, "Experimental Aesthetics," 301.

30 Ibid., 302.

EXACTITUDE AND ITS DISCONTENTS

FIGURE 8.1. A boy stands before the Probability Machine at Charles and Ray Eames's March 1961 exhibition *Mathematica: A World of Numbers . . . and Beyond* at the California Museum of Science and Industry. © Eames Office LLC (eamesoffice.com). All rights reserved.

Chapter 8
Filthy Logics

Exactitude and the Architecture of Mediocrity

Francesca Hughes

J'aime leur . . . leur illogisme . . . leur illogisme brûlant . . . cette flamme . . .
cette flamme . . . qui consume cette saloperie de logique.
—Samuel Beckett in conversation with Charles Juliet, 1977

In search of solace, I have recently returned to Samuel Beckett's *saloperie de logique,* and the many arch constructions of exacting pointlessness he designed to disarm it.[1] The assault on architectural education and practice by contemporary neoliberal "saloperies" is difficult to witness and even harder to fight. In the face of the current pincer grip of nineteenth-century statistics and digital solutionism that is increasingly scripting almost every dimension of our existence, revisiting Beckett reminds us that their alliance of construed inevitability is only ever that— construed.[2] In order to understand not only how but also why it is that this grip has achieved such swift and unchallenged purchase on our lives and the production of our cities, it is necessary to consider its manifest exactitude through the frame of big data's debt to the nineteenth century's most lasting architectural legacy, that of the bell-shaped curve that depicts the law of error, and its Rubin's vase–like flip to the capital "N" Normal curve, as it pivoted from a thinking about error-to-be-tolerated to a thinking about a-center-to-be-capitalized-upon—how to colonize indeterminacy in order to run an empire. Given that the law of error emerged from comparing readings in astronomy, it is perhaps unsurprising that, in the great ascendancy of social calculus, it was two astronomers that turned from their telescopes to measure the world: Adolphe Quetelet, who ultimately measures everything and in so doing effectively measures nothing; and Joseph Vallot, whose measure of a thing that evades all measure effectively measures measure itself. Both attend to the construction of a fundamental "filthy logic," to use Beckett's phrase. The history of the architecture of the bell-shaped curve, known variously as the Normal curve, law of error, or binominal or Gaussian distribution, is the history of a branch of mathematics whose saturation of all aspects of existence exceeded even that of calculus and is only recently being outstripped by big data, as its Victorian legacy comes home to roost.

To understand this legacy, we must return to Ian Hacking's extraordinary *Taming of Chance* (1990), newly relevant in uncanny ways, in which he recounts how the sacred pansophic projects of the Enlightenment were finally rendered profane in the nineteenth century, with its fever for measure and counting—the "avalanche of numbers" that saw to the beginnings of statistics, and the rendering of prediction industrialized.[3] In the projects of early statisticians, statistical laws came to be understood as laws in their own right, a new kind of "objective knowledge." In this first information age, nascent technologies for harvesting information fed these new kinds of laws, as prerevolution French rational moral science ceded to empirical moral science. Both architecture and the computer were there from the start. The first use of the term "constant," as a fixed value attached to an abstract property and thus a coefficient for a law, appeared in 1831 in a handbook of tables for tensile strengths of cast-iron beams and columns for architects and engineers. The next year, Charles Babbage proposed the collection of all "Constants of Nature and Art" and the counting of all things, including how much a man can saw in ten hours, elm, oak, or stone; the velocities of different birds; the heights of different buildings; the frequency of female children born out of wedlock; and the relative frequency of letters in different languages (Alan

Turing's cryptography in the wings)—all to fill his "granary of science," as if he somehow instinctively knew the progeny of his difference engines would have an insatiable appetite for data.[4]

Two of the stream of letters Adolphe Quetelet wrote to the Grand Duke of Saxe-Coburg and Gotha in *On the Theory of Probabilities as Applied to the Moral and Political Sciences* are important to any understanding of the all-conquering data artifice that was being constructed: one on his algorithm by which to predict the blooming of the lilac in a Brussels spring, and another regarding the distribution of "dwarfs" and "giants" in a given population. Both establish the norm and the average as (subtly) different but inseparable concepts—concepts to inevitably be rendered somehow "real."[5] Both are exquisite finger exercises in the data control that would master the colonies and then quietly underpin much of that which became infrastructural to the materialization of modernism (material sciences, standards and specifications, and identicality in mass production to name but a few manifestations), and ultimately guarantee the ascendency of big data.

Our first letter addresses that most capricious of events, the arrival of Spring, which Quetelet apparently brings to heel by the new scope of statistical measure: "Even the flower, so modest as it is, is not the product of a caprice of Nature: its frail tissue requires favourable conditions for its development; and to arrive at its full bloom, it follows laws as stable as those which preside over the progress of worlds."[6] Picking up where Linnaeus had apparently failed for "lack of precision," Quetelet set out to discover and fix the law by which to predict all lilac blossoming and render stable "this labyrinth where so many threads cross each other."[7] To this end all "threads," or variables, are systematically cut out of the picture, including that of the observers, themselves "a new cause of error," each with their propensity "to mark the epoch of blooming later than another." The flowering of *Syringa vulgaris* is (not without some eroticism) fixed as "that day on which the first corolla opens and shows the stamina."[8] All plants observed are to be equally healthy, aged, vigorous, fed, and positioned in equal soil and conditions. After just a few springs (such is the miracle of statistics) Quetelet is able to declare by induction that all lilacs in Brussels flower when the sum of the squares of the mean daily temperatures since the last frost reaches 4264 degrees centigrade. Quetelet's law of lilacs, like the fundamental laws it seeks to emulate, comprises an equation plus a constant, and thus endowed, like all laws, in predicting when lilacs will flower, the normative state, then establishes that which is deviant—tardy and premature lilacs and their host cities abound. Brussels becomes the prime meridian of global lilac blossoming. Other cities in the world are defined in terms of being in retardation to or in advance of Brussels' zero hour. However, to Quetelet's evident irritation, the new map of the world as defined by lilac behavior was unfortunately irregular: "The line which may be drawn through the globe, through all the places where a plant may flower on the same day (the isanthesic line), is not necessarily parallel to the line which passes through the places where this plant flowered ten or twenty days earlier."[9] If the law is to better meet deviation, it will need to admit more variables. Quetelet's attempt to align the blossoming of the lilac with the uniformity of Cartesian space reminds us that all measure is not measuring the real but *creating* the real, and doing so in order to then remeasure, control, and predict this new alias for the real.[10] Think of the curves we now consume daily and seek to "flatten," the "steps taken," to increase, that are our new "real." Think also of the innumerable real-time live data feeds, mediated by AI, that are holding sway in every aspect of our physical environment, not least its design—most recently in the form of software that provides "deep data insights" to the design process itself.[11] Suffice to say, Quetelet, Pierre-Simon Laplace, Francis Galton, and others' erection of the Normal curve, with its attendant statistical logics, was arguably the biggest infrastructural project of the nineteenth century—and it was virtual. Again, like big data, it had immediate concrete footprints in the rewriting of the world and its newly guaranteed predictability.

In our second letter, this time regarding the distribution of "dwarfs" and "giants," Quetelet's bizarre fixation with lilacs reveals its true ambitions. After lilac's denial of longitude, the size of man is brought to heel by Francis Galton's "Procrustean bed of the Law of Error" (Galton's words) with its (apparent) tolerance of deviation.[12] In a letter titled "Ordinary and Extraordinary Events— Monstrosities," Quetelet performs with size what he had performed with time in the case of lilacs, but with a crucial difference: seeking not the absolute resolution of calculation but the negotiated largesse of the bell curve. This time, the shoe (newly elasticated?) will fit. Do not, however, be fooled by the installation of generosity within the system; the corrective impulse remains: "I seek to give more exact appreciation to things to which everyone, according to his caprice, gives the most arbitrary values."[13]

The genius of the (filthy logic of the) Normal curve is its use of scale to temper, to the point of eradication, caprice—chance domesticated by probability. Quetelet discovered the miracle of distance: that zooming out in time and space effectively regulated all irregularities. As Georges Canguilhem formulated it in his *Le normal et le pathologique* (1966), "The greater the number of measurements carried out, the more the accidental disturbing causes will compensate and cancel out one and another and the more clearly the general type will appear."[14] In 1829 Quetelet had reported his "shock" at the "frightening regularity with which the same crimes are reproduced."[15] Regularity, or so it seems, was to be found not simply in rational events but also in events as irrational as crime, most especially the crime of suicide. Suicide, arguably the ultimate response to filthy logics, drove statistics. For Immanuel Kant, this new "political arithmetic" was no less than the discovery of "a natural purpose in this idiotic course of things human. . . . A history of a definite plan for creatures who have no plan of their own."[16] Ever the astronomer, Quetelet's response was that this mass regularity "shows that the laws of conservation can exist in the moral world, just as they are found in the physical world." Man is "restrained in such a circle, that the great laws of nature are forever exempted from his influence."[17] Like the planets, we too are trapped in an orbit, as we revolve around the commanding axis of the Normal. With a sufficiently big sample, births, marriages, deaths—all appeared to occur according to laws as immutable as those of the seasons. Obvious theological explanations followed.[18] However, the theological explanations were less obvious for the regularity of crimes, and even less so when presented with Pierre-Simon Laplace's discovery in 1827 that the number of dead letters in the Parisian postal system (letters that for whatever reasons never made it through the system or were returned) was constant from year to year.[19] Clearly god has a sense of humor. The French too: they put Laplace on a stamp.

It was not until Galton's description of the Normal curve in 1888 that François-Joseph Broussais and Auguste Comte's term "normal" (meaning typical) and Quetelet's curve (whose center denoted the space of the right and the good) inevitably came together. Galton's project was eugenics. This was a curve to be worshipped: "I know scarcely anything so apt to impress the imagination as the wonderful form of cosmic order expressed by the 'law of error.' A savage, if he could understand it, would worship it as a god. It reigns with *severity in complete self-effacement amidst the wildest confusion. The huger the mob and the greater the anarchy the more perfect is its sway.* Let a large sample of chaotic elements be taken and marshalled in order of their magnitudes, and then, however wildly irregular they appeared, an unexpected and most beautiful form of regularity proves to have been *present all along.*"[20] Its "self-effacement" means "its reign is invisible," "the greater the anarchy the more perfect its sway"—does this not sound newly familiar? In a later rendition of this statement Galton substitutes "the savage" with "the Ancient Greeks," in a move that echoes the inversion of the law of error to the Normal curve. The scope of this new law was breathtaking, not only was nothing, it seems, outside of its logic, which, as we are told, was "there all along," but upside down or inside out, it still decided all. It fitted everything: from Laplace's lost letters to Quetelet's giants and dwarfs to James Clerk Maxwell's distribution of molecular velocities in a gas to Galton's disappearance of the traits of genius in a family. Through its lens all in the world was trim, symmetrically distributed around a central axis, like the loading of cargo in the ships servicing the empire.

Quetelet invented the average man. His human "type," "from which the greater the divergence the rarer he is," is a canny bridge between the arithmetical average and the real. Quetelet's "typical" or "true" average, as opposed to the arithmetical average, is *designed* by chance itself, carved out of reality by the "unassignable multiplicity of nonsystematically oriented causes whose effects consequently tend to cancel out one another through progressive compensations."[21] Paradoxically it is precisely these "accidents" that would undo Quetelet's fundamental *type* and the divine laws behind them that he brings forth as evidence for their existence. As Canguilhem surmises, "If this were not the case, if men differed from one another—with respect to height for example—not because of the effect of accidental causes but because of the absence of a type with which they could be compared, no definite relationship could be established among all the individual measurements. On the other hand, if there is a type in terms of which divergences are purely accidental, a measured characteristic's numerical values, taken from any, many individuals, must be distributed according to a mathematical law and this is indeed what happens."[22]

Quetelet's *homme moyen* was also *l'homme moral*, and both had temporal dimensions scripting their rate of growth and rate of moral development. In the production of Quetelet's *homme moyen*, the measuring of limbs was fairly straightforward, but the measuring of the morality of *l'homme moyen moral* was more tricky—how to measure bravery, criminality, or amorousness? Quetelet acknowledges that while it would be possible to design a series of time-consuming, cross-referenced, complex experiments, one could instead simply record the number of brave, criminal, or amorous acts committed in a given year and then divide them by the number of the population, assigning the fraction as a *penchant* for criminality, et cetera, within *l'homme moyen moral*. André-Michel Guerry produced a map of the distribution of such penchants for France's departments, with Corsica winning as the hotbed of immorality, and even a moral computer or "ordonnateur statistique" to confirm his conclusions—anticipating the word "ordinateur" that IBM's Jacques Perrot introduces in France in 1955. Thus, through this simple act of reverse engineering, nineteenth-century data established the authority of the *exactitude of the inexact* that could even be, paradoxically, confirmed by mechanical calculation.

The exactitude of the inexact was thus enshrined by a double objectivity, that of data and that of the machine. Manifest today in more ways than we can even begin to count, as we find ourselves the subject of endless and invisible counting, the exactitude of the inexact has developed precocious rhetorical strategies. Think of the digital "nudge": such an innocent choice of word, so carefully cloaked in approximateness. The nudge is a calculated dialing back from what was once Facebook's clearly too pointy "poke"—all the better to conceal its utter confidence in its ability to persuade, to determine outcomes and change the course of events. Our decision making—for what is designing if not decision making—is being engineered like never before, and this engineering, like most engineering, owes more to the nineteenth century, Hacking's first information age, than the many accounts of the second information age care to admit.

If Quetelet made average height into something "real," as Hacking has argued, then Galton made correlation (partial causation or field causes) as real as cause. In 1930, Karl Pearson, in his monumental biography of his friend Galton, explained how the new autonomy of statistics, equipped with the new powers of correlation, undid causation: "The conception of causation—unlimitedly profitable to the physicist—began to crumble to pieces. In no case was B simply and wholly caused by A, nor indeed by C, D, E and F as well! It was really possible to go on increasing the number of contributory causes, until they might involve all the factors of the universe. The physicist was clearly picking out a few of the more important causes of A, and wisely concentrating on those. But no two physical experiments would—even if our instruments of measurement, men and machines, were perfect—ever lead to absolutely the same numerical result, because we could not include all the vast range of minor contributory causes. . . . Henceforward the philosophical view of the universe was to be that of a correlated system of variates, approaching but by no means reaching perfect correlation, i.e. absolute causality, even in the group of phenomena termed physical."[23] Galton's correlation for all intents and purposes killed cause. Such was the new autonomy of statistical law that it killed not only caprice at one end of the determinacy/indeterminacy spectrum—caprice that would undo the filthy logic of the bell curve—but also, at the other end, total determinism, the very idea of causality.[24] The neutralization of both, a necessary prerequisite for big data.

While Babbage's data harvest was to be stored for future use, Quetelet's was for present application, or, to be more precise, for the prediction of present futures. Nineteenth-century statisticians already understood, long before John von Neumann's "The part that is stable we are going to predict. And the part that is unstable we are going to control," that if you can explain something, you can control it, and if you can control it, you can predict it.[25] The autonomy that procures predictive power is always predicated on the ability of a model to explain the explananda it describes; explanatory power's first priority is always rhetorical; alignment to the truth or real is a secondary concern, indeed, a luxury. Such rhetorical power is best secured visually and repetitively, ideally via an animated model. For the Normal curve this was delivered by Galton's ingenious design of the quincunx, a glass-fronted box into which pellets of lead shot are dropped through openings in the top and fall through offset rows of pins—in quincunx formation, like the dots on the five side of a die—to always pile up at the bottom in a heap that traces a Normal curve, no matter how many iterations are played out: "The shot will all drop into the funnel, and running thence through its mouth, will pursue devious

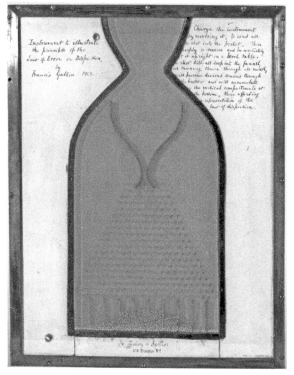

FIGURE 8.2. Sir Francis Galton's quincunx box, 1873. Copyright UCL Special Collections.

courses through the harrow and will accumulate in the vertical compartments at the bottom, there affording a representation of the law of dispersion."[26] In first presenting the device to the Royal Institution in 1893, Galton casts the pins or "spikes" off which the pellets deflect as simulating the "petty disturbances" of life. Their effects cancel each other out and, as with the type, the resolute curve appears below:

> The principle of the law of deviation is very simple. The important influences that acted upon each pellet were the same; namely, the position of the point whence it was dropped, and the force of gravity. So far as these are concerned, every pellet would have pursued an identical path. But in addition to these, there were a host of *petty disturbing influences,* represented by the spikes among which the pellets tumbled in all sorts of ways. The theory of combination shows that the commonest case is that where a pellet falls equally often to the right of a spike as to the left of it, and therefore drops into the compartment vertically below the point where it entered the harrow. It also shows that the cases are very rare of runs of luck carrying the pellet much oftener to one side of the successive spikes than the other. The law of deviation is purely numerical; it does not regard the fact whether the objects treated of are pellets in an apparatus like this, or shots at a target, or games of chance, or any other of the numerous groups of occurrences to which it is or may be applied.[27]

Crucial to the performance of the quincunx are the partition walls that separate the "compartments" and thus allow the curved heap of pellets to exceed the angle of repose, thus erasing gravity, materiality, and their geometry. This very clever rhetorical machine, with its harnessing of evident but invisible indeterminacy in order to make evident and visible the curve's ability to still determine all, employs strategic transparency (in every sense) in order to gain ideological purchase on logic and utility—this was the nineteenth century, after all, and there was a vast and complicated empire to be run. The perfection of the physicist was no longer the point. Utility and serviceableness were paramount: "Typical laws will never be exactly correct but at the same time will always be approximately true and always serviceable for explanation."[28] The quincunx or Galton Board, like the cloud chamber or the Van de Graaff generator (and I am tempted to add the guillotine to this list, but that is a different and longer story) as a seminal epistemic machine, renders "visible" and "comprehensible" that which is "invisible" and/or "incomprehensible." They do the explaining, so they own the truth. Among this family of epistemic machines, the quincunx is uniquely empowered, as it combines both of Peter Galison's two traditions: those that are image-based and make a picture of what they explain (the cloud or bubble chamber), and those that are logic-based and indexically demonstrate a theory through counting (as a Geiger counter does, for example, through the number of clicks), where one click means nothing, but a series of clicks tells a "statistical" story. The genius of the quincunx is that it does both—it "paints" a curve with the distribution of pellets that can also be counted, compartment by compartment.[29]

It is important to remember that this machine is also the machine

FIGURE 8.3. "*The Jewish Type*," 1878. Composite photographic portrait by Sir Francis Galton. The Galton Papers, UCL Library Services, Special Collections.

that is Galton's composite photographs of human *types*: private soldiers, murderers, the mentally ill, consumptives, Jews.[30] Galton commented that his composites were always "better looking than their components, because the averaged portrait of many persons is free from the irregularities that variously blemish the looks of each of them."[31] Their legacy is also the machine that is doing the "learning" in image recognition software, not least Google's, whose "unconscious" biases built into its algorithms identify a young woman of Afro-American descent as a "gorilla."[32] We know from Denis Diderot that overfitting has always been a dangerous business.[33] The irreducibility that delivers the universality of the universal law becomes, in statistical laws, their undisputed autonomy from any specificity that might challenge their epistemological security, or blemish their good looks. This very big picture, in its absorbing of all erratic data, is detail-proof. Similarly, all phenomena are accounted for, all external properties are disarmed. Caprice and causality neutralized, the final genius of statistics in its creation of the real is its elimination of any outside. Its exacting use of inexactness means that no phenomena can evade its elastic fit. It is the ultimate colonizer. Quetelet had always maintained that there should be a single method for all sciences, from mathematics to social sciences; this was to be it. Ultimately it is in this permeation of every aspect of life and thought that we find the keenest rehearsal of big data and the exacting inexactness of the technological solutionism it is deploying in apparently every corner of existence. This too is a closed system, and we are all trapped on the inside.

Whereas nineteenth-century industrialized data harvesting was to produce the identicality of the mass-produced for the standardized man, digital data harvesting has produced the differentiality of the customized subjects who are, ultimately, all similarly different, according to Quetelet's "host of petty influences," and so, for all intents and purposes, all the same.[34] So compelling is Galton's epistemic machine that it secures the institution of its logics for good. This machine does not evolve because it does not need to—in its substitution of perfection it is already perfect. An eleven-foot-high iteration is made by Charles and Ray Eames, and labeled "Galton's Probability Board" for their 1961 *Mathematica* exhibition, where it is positioned like an altar, center stage. Then in 1964 the

FIGURE 8.4. Charles and Ray Eames with their model of the *Mathematica* exhibition, 1961. The Probability Machine is at the center, below Ray's hand. © Eames Office LLC (eamesoffice.com). All rights reserved.

epistemic performance of the Galton Board meets that of the computer in their IBM Pavilion designed with Eero Saarinen for the World's Fair. The Eames placed a giant board, renamed "Probability Machine," at the entrance, where it stood sentinel. In their 1965 film *IBM: At the Fair*, it is shown with crowds flocking around it, worshipping (whether like savages or ancient Greeks is unclear) the cascade of pellets through its spikes. The camera zooms in, and pellets dart left and right as they bounce off the spikes to Elmer Bernstein's staccato piano score. The crowd are held in suspense as they watch the making of mediocrity:

FIGURE 8.5. Frame enlargements from *IBM at the Fair,* Charles and Ray Eames, 1965, 7 mins. © Eames Office LLC (eamesoffice.com). All rights reserved.

> A number of small and independent accidents befall each shot in its career. In rare cases, a long run of luck continues to favour the course of a particular shot toward either outside place, but in the large majority of instances the number of accidents that cause Deviation to the right, balance in a greater or less degree those that cause Deviation to the left. Therefore, most of the shot finds its way into the compartments that are situated near to a perpendicular line drawn from the outlet of the funnel, and the Frequency with which shots stray to different distances to the right or left of that line diminishes in a much faster ratio than those distances increase. This illustrates and explains the reason why mediocrity is common.[35]

In the very same year that Galton was presenting his machine to the Royal Institution, our second astronomer, Joseph Vallot, was setting to the measurement of that most capricious object, the glacier—a landscape so evasive of measure that its very landmarks, the giant granite boulders it carries within its shape-shifting mantle, not only move but are named "erratics." Vallot, however, was cunning. He understood that in the taming of the glacier, only the glacier could measure the glacier. And this via a peculiar forward engineering of the reverse engineering that is the study of erratics: the deposited boulder is here, therefore the glacier passed through here, therefore it started there. Vallot's method is disarmingly simple: he lays four lines of brightly painted and numbered stones across the glacier. Each line is then surveyed and plotted onto a map. Each successive September 15 the stones are refound and resurveyed. Thus, the glacier becomes a self-measuring machine as the stones, ever so slowly, fall with and through it, tracking its very slow descent. This glacier as self-measuring machine is also a self-explaining machine, translating the white noise of its unpredictable surface into the regular curved wave fronts that span its width. The trim of velocities around its central axis is installed—fastest at the glacier's center, slowest at its edges. The glacier is a live, supine, curved data set, and, thus tamed, a magnificent epistemic machine that can predict itself.

But this machine is not so compliant. Vallot describes in anxious detail how each summer his cohort of agents would scurry across the irregular icy surface, installing the line of stones onto which they paint their allocated integer before the line is left to its own devices— *abandonnée à elle-même,* as his journal records—or to the devices of the glacier whose progress swallows up the stones into its ever-reconfiguring pockets. Less like the pellets in the quincunx than the letters in the Parisian postal service, the stones and their lines are left to find, or fall, their way through the system. Each September the game of hunt the line of-stones would resume: "This hunting of the stones obsessed us and we would search out our quarry with fervent ardour, leaping across enormous crevasses, climbing the sharpest, most slicing arêtes, unroped, each unto themselves, in order to search as wide a surface as possible."[36] There were, however, certain terrains that the stones had entered, where, defeated by topography,

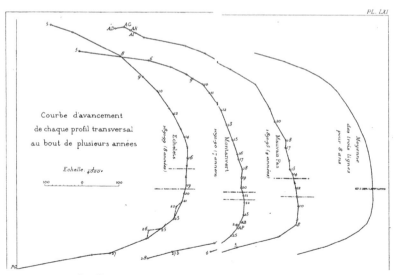

FIGURE 8.6. Joseph Vallot's drawing of the Mer de Glace's progress, 1900. Courtesy of Bibliothèque nationale de France, département Sciences et techniques, 4-V-3740.

Vallot and his men could not follow: "In the ice cascades . . . all the seracs had formed into needle-like peaks . . . and one would scarcely find an odd stone balanced on the peak of an arête, almost all having rolled down into the depths of the crevasses."[37]

Certain stones disappeared in the system for years at a time before the glacier finally returned them to the surface. Vallot and his team of stone hunters soon learned to outlast the glacier's game of hide-and-seek, calculating that a stone that had fallen into an eight-meter-deep crevasse would be exposed at the surface again two summers later. Faced with a capricious subject, this system of measure acquires a certain craftiness in order to install regularity. Is this the first sign of the beginning of the end of its authority? The cooking of the statistical books? The analogue "nudge"? In Vallot's plotting of the glacier's velocity curve, what isomorphic desires drive his need to find every stone within this practice of measure? Does the missing stone/the thwarted measure not also count within this survey?

The character Molloy in Samuel Beckett's novel by the same name is similarly possessed by a set of needs relating to stones and pockets and their counting. His sixteen sucking stones are, following "the principle of trim," distributed equally across his body: four in each of the two pockets on the right-hand side (coat and trousers), four in the two on his left-hand side.[38] Thus loaded, Molloy is a closed system as he sucks the stones one at a time in rotation, clockwise, from coat pocket to mouth to coat pocket to trouser pocket to trouser pocket.

After a while, however, he comes to the disturbing realization that his system is not safe: that caprice could enter and sabotage its logics, that by "an extraordinary hazard, the four stones circulating thus might always be the same four." This hazard soon becomes intolerable: such a system "could not long content a man like me . . . the truth is I should have needed sixteen pockets in order to be quite easy on my mind. . . . For I was beginning to lose all sense of measure."[39] An outfit of sixteen pockets being quite impossible, Molloy considers the only alternative, echoing Vallot: that of numbering the stones. But this too has drawbacks. Tracking of the numbers requires the bureaucracy of accounting that Babbage and Quetelet poured down their numerical avalanche. "No, the only perfect solution would have been the sixteen pockets, symmetrically disposed each one with its stone. Then I would have needed neither to number nor to think, but merely, as I sucked a given stone, to move on to the fifteen others."[40] Neither to number, nor to think—doing one thing at a time, like Turing's tape—Molloy, in his processing cycles, must behave like a computer.

Inevitably Vallot's system too starts to leak and let caprice in as the lines embark on their own misadventures. The Échelet line encounters a region full of crevasses and loses its right flank, stones one to thirteen, except for stone five and stone eight. Another loses its left flank after suddenly falling into a series of icefalls; the next year, most of these stones reappear. But then in 1898, the Montavert line's stones nine to fourteen get lost in a zone of enormous, sharp waves—all falling to the bottom of the deepest pockets of the crevasses, only to reappear in 1899 on the Rochers des Mottets.

Molloy soon realizes that he must make a sacrifice: "And while I gazed thus at my stones, revolving interminable martingales all equally defective . . . it suddenly dawned on the former [his mind], dimly, that I might perhaps achieve my purpose without increasing the number of my pockets, or reducing the number of my stones, *but simply sacrificing the principle of trim*."[41]

The "sacrifice" is aesthetic—remember the beauty of Galton's composite portraits that made manifest the seduction of the curve that was there all along, behind the chaos. His elegant system is rendered ugly as trim is abandoned and he loads himself asymmetrically. "Here it is in all its hideousness": Molloy puts six stones in the right pocket of his greatcoat, the newly designated "supply pocket," the left coat pocket is empty, and both trouser pockets have five stones; he sucks all six from the right coat pocket one by one, transferring them to the left coat pocket. When the right coat pocket is empty, he rotates the contents of all pockets one pocket clockwise, resetting the system, then continues the subcycle as above, resetting whenever the supply pocket is empty, ad infinitum.[42]

Only this way can Molloy be sure that all sixteen stones "will have been sucked at least once, in impeccable succession, not one sucked twice, not one left unsucked. But this solution is not without a price: the abandoning of trim "was painful to me, bodily. . . . I felt the weight of the stones dragging me now to one side, now to the other." But the need to suck the stones in a way that was "not haphazard, but with method was also, I think a bodily need. Here then were two incompatible bodily needs at loggerheads."[43]

Molloy's "loggerhead" is the meeting of measure that attempts to access the real with measure that seeks to replace the real, of measure that actually measures with measure that *looks like* it measures, the tension between precision true to its purpose and an aesthetic of precision, of exactitude fetishized to the point of being divorced from both subject and purpose. This tension is not unlike that between veridicality (explanatory power) and veracity (alignment with the truth) in our family of seminal epistemic machines. The Mer de Glace did not satisfy Vallot's bodily needs either. The cache of orphaned colored stones lost in its secret linings with fading numbers on their faces are testimony to the anxious industry of nineteenth-century measure getting ready for the twentieth- and now the twenty-first century's big data.

Beckett's many industrious attempts to design wholly pointless actions and systems that, to paraphrase his edict on inexpression, do nothing, with nothing, from nothing, to nothing, for nothing, speak acutely to the practice of measure and to the exactitude, including the exactitude of the inexact, to which it attends.[44] As Beckett understood, the design of a project of pure pointlessness is the most difficult and most important thing to achieve, a project of "burning illogicality—the flame . . . which consumes all our filthy logic." Molloy's attempt to design such a system—his anxious perfecting of its abject pointlessness—is ultimately sabotaged by his nostalgia for the principle of trim, for the filthy logic of symmetry's normal curve. Thus, we are reminded that any project of exactitude is not simply about the power and control that quantification procures but is also always an aesthetic project, and vice versa.[45] Any practice of measure is doomed to occupy this space of conflict between genuine engagement with the object and the measuring subject's autoseduction by the aestheticization of method and its registers—always an own goal that leaves us, like Molloy, contentedly sucking yet deluded.

Beckett's revolving martingales that sabotage Molloy's delusion represent the caprice that would not be tamed. In the same year that Galton made his quincunx, and Vallot plants numbered stones in the glacier, American philosopher and surveyor of the US coastline C. S. Peirce writes this: "Chance itself pours in at every avenue of sense: it is of all things the most obtrusive. That it is absolute is the most manifest of all intellectual perceptions. That it is a being, living and conscious, is what all the dullness that belongs to ratiocination's self can scarce muster the hardihood to deny."[46]

The Galton Board surfaces again, in the basement of Princeton's School of Engineering and Applied Sciences, in the PEAR lab (the Princeton Engineering Anomalies Research) in 1979. There it is subjected to tests in psychokinesis as operators attempt to engage with "a being, living and conscious" and to free caprice (and causality) from Galton's trim-induced probability (and correlation) by willing the balls to fall asymmetrically. Reincarnated as the Random Mechanical Cascade, it now comprises nine thousand polystyrene balls, a matrix of 330 pegs in quincunx formation, and nineteen collecting bins. The experiment in question "calls for the operator, seated on a couch about eight feet from the machine, to attempt to distort the distribution of balls to the right or higher numbered bins, or to the left or lower numbered bin, or to generate a base line. These intentions (left or right) are interspersed in concomitant sets of three runs, each of which lasts about 12 minutes."[47] It is observed that some operators produce differing results depending on whether the choice of left or right intention is theirs or is randomly assigned. It is also noticed that first-timers produce more extreme results.

FIGURE 8.7. A random mechanical cascade experiment under way at PEAR lab, Princeton, 1980s. Courtesy of the International Consciousness Research Laboratories (ICRL).

In an interview years later, the laboratory manager Brenda Dunne explained that the operators "may not look like they're doing much, but they're trying to influence the output of these machines with their minds. The ones who get the best results don't think too hard about it."[48]

The scientists note that women get "larger results" than men, but often in the direction they did not intend. Two people working together do better than a lone operator. A man and a woman in a relationship produce startling results. However, when groups of local elementary school children tour the lab, the outcome "is off the charts."[49]

Princeton closed down the lab in 2007.

NOTES

1 "I like their illogicality, their burning illogicality—the flame . . . which consumes all our filthy logic." Charles Juliet, *Rencontres avec Samuel Beckett*, e-book (Paris: Editions P.O.L, 2011), 58. Paper ed., *Nouvelle Imprimerie Laballery*, 2007.

2 Digital solutionism is big data deployed as the quick fix that eternally postpones addressing the root causes of a problem while systematically rejecting political alternatives. Evgeny Morozov's prediction that the COVID-19 pandemic will do for the solutionist state what 9/11 did for the surveillance state is fast becoming confirmed. "Neoliberalism shrinks public budgets; solutionism shrinks public imagination. The solutionist mandate is to convince the public that the only legitimate use of digital technologies is to disrupt and revolutionise everything but the central institution of modern life—the market." Evgeny Morozov, "The Tech 'Solutions' for Coronavirus Take the Surveillance State to the Next Level," *Guardian*, April 15, 2020, https://www.theguardian.com/commentisfree/2020/apr/15/tech-coronavirus-surveilance-state-digital-disrupt.

3 Ian Hacking, *The Taming of Chance* (Cambridge: Cambridge University Press, 1990).

4 Charles Babbage, "Mr Babbage on the Constant of Nature and Art," *Edinburgh Journal of Science* 12 (1832): 340.

5 In Georges Canguilhem's analysis, what Quetelet sets up in the concept of the norm is a "meaning analogous to that of the concept of the type which Quetelet had superimposed on his theory of the average man following the discovery of the true average. It is an analogous meaning that is similar in function but different in foundation." Georges Canguilhem, *The Normal and the Pathological* (New York: Zone Books, 1991), 262.

6 M. A. Quetelet, *Letters Addressed to H.R.H. the Grand Duke of Saxe-Coburg and Gotha, On the Theory of Probabilities: As Applied to the Moral*

and Political Sciences, trans. O. G. Downes (London: Charles and Edwin Layton, 1849), 156.

7   M. A. Quetelet, *On the Theory of Probabilities,* 157. Research on the blooming of the gooseberry, willow, birch, and poplar in Linnaeus's *Aménités académiques* was abandoned as no conclusion could be drawn from it. In Quetelet's assessment there were "inexplicable discordances" in his numbers because he "had not made his question sufficiently precise" (166).

8   Ibid., 158.

9   Ibid., 173.

10 As Georges Canguilhem, quoting Claude Bernard, points out, the average does not exist: "For example the analysis of average urine over a 24 hour period is 'the analysis of a urine which does not exist.'" Canguilhem, *Normal and Pathological,* 152.

11 Recent AI applications that combine information metrics with form finding for property developers such as *Archistar,* which "helps property professionals to find profitable development sites, assess for feasibility and generate dozens of architectural design strategies—all within a few minutes," and *Blox,* whose platform's dashboard incorporates "real time adjustable inputs, deep data insights," allowing a developer to "project assets and financials" adding "live data enables rapid decisions," are just two recent manifestation of the flow of real time data currently feeding the "filthy logics" at work in the making architecture. Antonio Pacheco, "Gensler Launches Blox, an Algorithm-Powered Design Visualization and Computation Tool," *Archinect News,* June 16, 2020, https://archistar .ai, https://archinect.com/news/article/150202814/gensler-launches-blox -an-algorithm-powered-design-visualization-and-computation-tool.

12 In 1877 Francis Galton wrote to H. P. Bowditch, advising him to force his anthropometric data into "the Procrustean bed of the law of error." Galton quoted in Hacking, *Taming of Chance,* 184.

13 Quetelet, *On the Theory of Probabilities,* 102.

14 Canguilhem, *Normal and Pathological,* 157.

15 M. A. Quetelet, "Recherches Statistiques," in Theodore M. Porter, *The Rise of Statistical Thinking, 1820–1900* (Princeton, NJ: Princeton University Press, 1986), 49.

16 Immanuel Kant in Porter, *Rise of Statistical Thinking,* 50.

17 Porter, *Rise of Statistical Thinking,* 52.

18 "For me the principal idea is to cause the truth to prevail and to show how much man, without his knowledge, is subject to divine laws and with what regularity he realises them. Moreover, his regularity is not peculiar to man: it is one of the great laws of nature belonging to animals as well as plants and it will be surprising perhaps that it was not recognized sooner." Quetelet quoted in Canguilhem, *Normal and Pathological,* 158.

19 "The ratios of the acts of nature are very nearly constant when these acts are considered in great number. Thus, in spite of the variety of years the sum of the productions during a considerable number of years is sensibly the same; so that man by useful foresight is able to provide against the

irregularity of the seasons by spreading out equally over all the seasons the goods which nature distributes in an unequal manner. I do not except from the above law results due to moral causes. The ratio of annual births to the population, and that of marriages to births, show only small variations; at Paris the number of annual births is almost the same, and I have heard it said at the post-office in ordinary seasons the number of letters thrown aside on account of defective addresses changes little each year; this has likewise been observed at London." Pierre-Simon Laplace, *A Philosophical Essay on Probabilities,* trans. Andrew I. Dale (Berlin: Springer-Verlag, 1995), chap. 8, para. 62.

20 Galton's "Presidential Address," *Journal of the Anthropological Institute* 15 (1886): 494.

21 Georges Canguilhem, *Normal and Pathological*, 156.

22 Ibid., 157.

23 Karl Pearson, *The Life, Letters, and Labours of Francis Galton* (Cambridge: Cambridge University Press, 1930), vol. 3A, chap. 14, 2.

24 This death was ultimately sealed by cybernetics. In 1800, prior to the development "the social calculus" or "social physics," the word "chance" denoted fortune or possibly lawlessness. Any event was understood to have followed from a chain of causation that could explain it. Chance, newly domesticated by probability and thus newly "predictable," was deemed less capricious than chaos. Curiously the new meaning of "chance" emerged at the same time as the new meaning of the word "precision" as it changed from the eighteenth-century's sense of asymptotically homing in on an absolute value (the sharpness of a needle, for instance) to the sense of predictability (the identicality of mass-produced needles). Again, we see the nineteenth century paving the way for big data.

25 George Dyson, *Turing's Cathedral: The Origins of the Digital Universe* (London: Penguin Press, 2013), 154.

26 This is a transcription of Galton's handwritten instructions on the front of his quincunx.

27 Francis Galton, "Typical Laws of Heredity," *Proceedings of the Royal Institution*, vol. 8, weekly evening meeting of Friday February 9, 1877, 289; emphasis mine.

28 Francis Galton in his lecture to the Royal Institution in which he first presented his quincunx. As Hacking points out, curiously C. S. Peirce, in the same decade, was also developing his quincuncial projection for cartographic purposes. See Hacking, *Taming of Chance*, 180.

29 See Peter Galison, "Epistemic Machines: Image and Logic," in *When Is the Digital in Architecture?*, ed. Andrew Goodhouse (Montreal/Berlin: CCA and Sternberg Press, 2017).

30 Galton's composite photographic portraits, using a technique he developed in the 1880s, were made by multiple exposure onto the same photographic plate of different subjects, always aligning the eyes.

31 Galton quoted in Porter, *Rise of Statistical Thinking*, 140.

32 Alarmingly, Google's quick fix was to ban the word "gorilla" from its Photos app. "Google Apologises for Photos App's Racist Blunder," Technology pages, *BBC News,* July 1, 2015, https://www.bbc.com/news/technology-33347866.

33 Diderot concluded the *Encyclopédie* he edited with Jean-Baptiste le Rond d'Alembert with a prescient caution against the illusory nature of all that was inferred from data analysis: "These methodological divisions aid the memory and seem to control the chaos formed by the objects of nature. . . . But one should not forget that these systems are based on arbitrary human conventions, and do not necessarily accord with the invariable laws of nature." Denis Diderot and Jean-Baptiste le Rond d'Alembert, "Histoire Naturelle," in *Encyclopédie*, vol. 7 (Paris: André le Breton, 1751), 230.

34 Francis Galton, "Typical Laws of Heredity," 289.

35 Francis Galton, *Natural Inheritance* (New York: Macmillan, 1894), 63–65.

36 "Cette chasse à la pierre nous passionnait, et nous cherchions notre gibier avec ardeur, sautant par-dessus d'énormes crevasses, gravissant les arêtes les plus tranchantes, sans corde, chacun de son côté, pour explorer une plus grande surface"; translation mine. Joseph Vallot, "Expériences sur la marche et les variations de la Mer de Glace," *Annales de l'Observatoire Météorologique du Mont-Blanc* (Paris: G Steinheil, 1900), vol. 4, chap. 4, "Marches des Lignes de Pierres Peintes," 79.

37 "Dans les régions où le glacier était coupé en forme de damier par des crevasses verticales, larges et profondes, il était impossible d'avancer. De même dans les cascades de glace où tous les séracs sont en forme d'aiguilles. Les regions couvertes d'arêtes aiguës étaient accessibles, mais il était bien rare d'y trouver quelque pierre perchée au sommet d'une arête, presque tout ayant roulé au fond des crevasses"; translation mine. Vallot, *Expériences sur la Marche,* 79.

38 Samuel Beckett, *Three Novels: Molloy, Malone Dies, The Unnamable* (New York: Grove Press, 1958).

39 Ibid., 64–65.

40 Ibid., 68.

41 "Martingale" refers to a surprisingly simple betting strategy that emerged in the 1930s whose ultimate aim was to show that without infinite iterations (time) or infinite resource (money), all such strategies necessarily fail—all our endeavors to make sense of or measure the chaos of our godless universe are doomed. In the later sense of the term in probability theory, the physical model of a martingale is Brownian motion, another epistemic machine and a figure that is echoed in the second part of *Molloy* by Moran's description of his bees and "the complexity of their innumerable dance"; emphasis mine. Both strategy and model rehearse Beckett's preoccupation with contemporary uncertainty theory. Beckett, *Three Novels*, 66.

42 Beckett, *Three Novels*, 66–67. It is worth reading the perfected tedium with which Beckett describes his "hideous" asymmetrical process, a lengthy passage that is simultaneously exquisite and as dull as "ditchwateristics" to employ Dickens's term for statistics.

43 Ibid., 67–68.

44 "The expression that there is nothing to express, nothing with which to express, nothing from which to express, no power to express, no desire to express, together with the obligation to express." Samuel Beckett and Georges Duthuit "Three Dialogues: Tal Coat Masson—Bram Van Velde," *Transition* 49, 5 (Dec. 1949): 97–103.

45 I am indebted to my most dear, and now late, friend and colleague Mark Cousins for pointing out to me the pointlessness of all aesthetic endeavors.

46 C. S. Peirce, "Reply to Necessitarians" (1893), quoted in Hacking, *Taming of Chance*, 200.

47 Roger Nelson, Brenda Dunne, Robert G. Jahn, "Operator-Related Anomalies in a Random Mechanical Cascade," *Journal of Scientific Exploration* 2, no. 2 (1988): 155–79.

48 Brenda J. Dunne, laboratory manager at PEAR since its inception in 1979, quoted in J. D. Reed, "Mind Over Matter," *New York Times*, March 9, 2003, https://www.nytimes.com/2003/03/09/nyregion/mind-over-matter.html.

49 Ibid.

Chapter 9

The In-Exact Words of Architecture

Teresa Stoppani

In-exact

There are words in architecture that endure beyond definitions, cultures, and times. Because they don't change, they change. They are malleable, elastic, they reset themselves again and again, to adhere to something that changes continuously—life. It is because they don't change that they change. Here I suggest that the *in*-exact words of architecture open up a crucial space between the word and the thing/space, in which the project becomes possible and remains active. The words that endure allow us to plot continuities and transformations and to work through adaptations and permanence, because we continue to use them, across languages, cultures, and geographies. Translation further opens up the space of potentiality for the project, as a word takes on new meanings and sheds other meanings in its journeys, encounters, and returns. It is the words that attach themselves to the changeable and the unnamable that last longer: because they change, they don't change.

A discussion of exactitude in relation to architecture and the city begs for a rethinking of "exactitude" from within, to embrace what is only apparently its opposite. I call it the *in*-exact. In-exactitude is not imprecision, sloppiness, or carelessness. On the contrary, the in-exact is a careful opening, a suspension, and an invitation at once. It is also a possibility. It allows for a suspension that opens to interpretation and to a change that does not need to be tracked, traced, and controlled. It is the hypothetical of the "what if," the curiosity of a "let's see." It is the space for a questioning that allows for the possibility of change.

Italo Calvino's invitation to exactitude in his *Six Memos for the Next Millennium* is a gradual approach, a careful job of skimming, scraping and cleaning it from its incrustations, to arrive at a practice rather than a definition.[1] Giacomo Leopardi's words on the vague and the indefinite in the *Zibaldone* are his starting point. As the poet argues, one can speak of the vague and the indefinite only if this is done with exactitude: "A highly exact and meticulous attention to the composition of each image, to the minute definition of details, to the choice of objects, to the lighting and the atmosphere, all in order to attain the desired degree of vagueness."[2] Robert Musil, another master of grasping the indefinite, is also one of the key references in Calvino's approach to exactitude. Musil writes about exactitude as an intellectual habit that produces "a human being with the paradoxical combination of precision and indefiniteness."[3]

It is exactitude's "combination of precision and indefiniteness" that invites us to rethink it from with-in, to open it up and expose its "paradoxical" combinations. A consideration of exactitude as a combination of precision and indefiniteness in relation to architecture opens architecture to possibility and to change. It unfolds architecture's relational dimension as a discipline (in constant transformation), as a project (and its influences, contexts, and collaborations), and as an edifice (designed and made to be inhabited, transgressed, transformed, and maintained). It also means that architecture cannot exist alone. Invested with meanings, uses, and perceptions, architecture does not coincide (it does not end) with its object. It communicates.

Like architecture, this text oscillates: from architecture to the city and back, and again. This too is a space of *in*-exactitude, a movement that transverses and transgresses definitions and boundaries, redefining at each turn. Oscillating between "precision and indefiniteness," the fragments below suggest the crucial openness that certain in-exact words of the architectural language contain. In their changing permanence, the vibrations of "Type" and the oscillations of "City" allow for the construction (or rediscovery) of ephemeral continuities, identifications, and inventions, thus allowing architecture to "go on."

The operations of architecture's in-exact words are both precise and identifiable, yet they too move, between language and image, form and space. The translation and placing (Beckett) and the extraction (Calvino) of words; the imperfection (Calvino) and the oscillation (Barthes) of literary images; the naming (Quatremère de Quincy) and un-naming (De Boeck) of architecture and the city; the un-naming and renaming (Calvino) and the undoing and infinity (Piranesi) of the city, and its moving and opening (Cacciari); the dismissing (Metapolis Institute), suspension (Sassen), and recovering (Kwinter) of the city—these are the leaps proposed here to perform the in-exactitude of architecture and of the city. The links—acrobatic or smooth, obvious, personal, invisible, intended, invented—are left to the reader, architect, and citizen.

Unplaceable

> You must say words, as long as there are any, until they find me . . . where I am, I don't know, I'll never know . . . , in the silence you don't know, you must go on, I can't go on, I'll go on.
> —Samuel Beckett, *The Unnamable*

"Where now? Who now? When now?"[4] These are the words with which Samuel Beckett begins his questioning in *The Unnamable,* an interrogation in which the "I" is endlessly iterated, constantly probed, yet remains the most unfathomable presence in the novel.[5] The unnamable narrator, "so named because he knows not who he may be," is the one we get to know in the novel, while he continues to wonder/wander "where," "who," "when." The Aristotelian categories of place, time, and action are acknowledged but also dissolved. Yet the impossibility of (ever) knowing frames those repeated "now, now, now" at the beginning as a "next," as a possibility and an impossibility, as a compulsion toward a future of change and of questioning, in which, because "I'll never know . . . I'll go on."

Beckett wrote and published *The Unnamable* in French first, as *L'innommable*, in 1953. He then spent more time translating the novel than he had spent writing it. And the translation is a rewriting, a transformation. One of the changes that occur at the very beginning of the text, "somewhat less logically?" according to Steven Connor,[6] is the slipping of the unfathomable "I": in the English version the "who" (*qui*) is moved in-between "where" (*où*) and "when" (*quand),* sliding now in-between place and time. The French "*Où maintenant? Quand maintenant? Qui maintenant?*" becomes in the English version "Where now? Who now? When now?" The "I" is thus set into motion, relating to place and time, but also questioning and redefining them, in a set of movable relations.

Exígere

"Exact," in its verb form "to exact," from the Latin *exígere,* expresses an inner demand more than an imposed requirement.[7] *Ex-agĕre* is first of all a pushing out from within, before exactitude becomes something of a requirement, or an expectation. Indeed, the motivation we find in Italo Calvino's lecture "Exactitude" comes from within, and his American lessons (*Lezioni americane* is the Italian title of his *Six Memos for the Next Millennium*) are at once a literary autobiographical account and the gift of a legacy, to other writers, but also to us, who compose, assemble, design, imagine, and always approximate.[8] What Calvino teaches us is the value of our approximations, and the fact that they do not approximate a given something, or a something to achieve, but work with it and with-in it. Exactitude is in the work of those approximations. Exactitude is not perfection. Calvino's *Six Memos* are not six but five, because death intervenes to exact us from ourselves.[9] Even in dying we are not perfect.

Imperfect

The "Exactitude" memo begins with an oscillation. Calvino opens with a reference to Maat, the Egyptian goddess of the scales, who was symbolized "by a feather that served as a weight on scales used for the weighing of souls."[10] Yet Maat the feather is also twofold. Her hieroglyph, Calvino explains, stands "for a unit of length" and also "for the fundamental note of the flute": that is, a reference that measures and is repeated, and one that is a starting point. Different ways to keep deviation in check. Different behaviors.

From there the memo or lesson unfolds, giving us a methodology and a perfect example of a text whose meanderings are integral and crucial to its argumentation. Ultimately, the text oscillates between Maat the measurer and Maat the trigger (of imagination, of composition, of work). Calvino moves from Leopardi's attempt in the *Zibaldone* to define vagueness through word images, where "the search for the indefinite becomes the observation of all that is multiple, teeming, composed of countless particles," to Leonardo's three versions of the description of an animal, a sort of sea monster he is interpreting from its fossilized remains, which becomes in fact a conjecture of how the animal moves in the sea—"looming," "swirling," "furrowing."[11] Exactitude is not a static affair but a pursuit destined for and aiming at failure—that is, if nonfailure means perfection.

Oscillation

> The overcoming of the conflictual doesn't occur through suspension, abstention, abolition of the paradigm, but through invention of a third term: complex term and not zero, neutral term.
> —Roland Barthes, *The Neutral*

Calvino's "Exactitude" memo includes a reference to Roland Barthes, "in whose mind—he writes—the demon of exactitude lived side by side with the demon of sensitivity."[12] Here, Calvino is thinking of Barthes's claim for a *mathesis singularis* rather than a *mathesis universalis* in *La chambre claire* (*Camera Lucida*). But it is in his lectures on the "Neutral" that Barthes discusses the "virtues" of oscillation as hesitation, seen here not as paralyzing or stalling but as the space for "the more agreeable, the unexpected that could occur," and both as "functioning as an objective device, not like a 'disorder', an anomie, a difficult margin, but, all being said, like a reconquest, a stabilization, a working on one's image." Barthes sees the Neutral as "a discourse . . . and as such a 'screen' or rather a 'noise,' through which something is being said by the subject, unknowingly or knowingly but unacknowledgedly."[13]

The section on "Oscillation" in Barthes's lecture (of May 6, 1978) could almost be read as the continuation or complement to Calvino's lecture on Exactitude: "It's by confronting related words that one refines meanings, differences, nuances . . . nuance is one of the linguistic tools of non-arrogance, of non-intolerance."[14] Here Barthes probes the different meanings of the three ancient Greek words that indicate different forms of the Neutral: "The grammatical Neutral: to *oudétéron* (neither one nor the other). . . . The political Neutral: leans on no side: *mésos* (middle). . . . A third, more interesting word: *hétéroklitos*: (a) he who leans on one side and the other; (b) grammar: words whose declension proceeds from different themes, 'irregular' words . . . the irregular, the unforeseeable, of one following the other without order."[15]

[Yet-]unnamed

Nous proposons de nous concentrer dès à présent sur le non dénommé.
—Lieven De Boeck, "Typology," in *Seven Sins of Urbanism*

Im-perfection, oscillation, and in-exactitude characterize those words that we use in architecture, and continue to use even when what they refer to changes, has changed, is changing. They are elastic words, capable of stretching over and embracing that which is changing, new, surprising, planned yet uncontrollable. They feign stability, roofing over mutations that both corrode and enrich an origin that often we cannot find, because it is not one but many, already.

As defined by Quatremère de Quincy, Type is form-less and "more or less vague." Type is a nucleus for a complexity of spatial arrangements that are adaptable to—but are not (or not only) generated by—function. It is not a static form but a multiplicity of variations. Type operates in time "like a sort of nucleus about which are collected, and to which are co-ordinated *in time*, the developments and *variations of forms* to which the object is susceptible,"[16] as Quatremère notes. Generative flexibility, vagueness, and nonrepresentativity characterize Type as a flexible tool that is in-formative rather than formal, and that cannot be represented as a form but only as an interpretative accumulation of constantly shifting forms, molded according to the occasion to perform as critical agents. The vagueness inherent in Quatremère's definition of Type questions the stability of form and opens the classical language of architecture to the oscillations of the multiple.

In *The Seven Sins of Urbanism* (2002), Lieven De Boeck denounces the seven "sins" of modernist urbanism.[17] His table titled "Typology" (statement #5 0903) advocates the "suppression" of the notion of typology, of the modernist "form follows function" and function separation, to produce a "more attractive world" made of the nondenominate. The statement implicitly refers back to the much wider and yet architecturally more precise notion of Type as developed by the architectural theorists of the Enlightenment. The fluid and recombinable—and yet precise—arrangement of the new "nondenominate" can be traced back to the roots of the Type, with all its potentials for reelaboration and only partial adhesion or total indifference to the issue of function. Named and renamed, contents, arrangements, and selectively permeable boundaries find a better nondefinition in the unnamable flowing fixity of Type. In De Boeck's manifesto, the attractiveness of the *non-dénommé* derives from its challenging of function: the modernist language of architecture is subjected to even wider oscillations, as it questions the given of function and incorporates the unexpected or the yet-unnamed.

Improbable

> By reducing the number of abnormal elements, we increase the probability that such a city exists.
> —Italo Calvino, *Invisible Cities*

In reflecting on exactitude as oscillation, Calvino inevitably comes to consider the city as a complex site of tension: it is the city that that gives "greater possibilities of expressing the tension between geometric rationality and the entanglements of human lives."[18] About his book *Invisible Cities,* he explains, "I built up a many-faceted structure in which each brief text is close to the others in a series that does not imply logical sequence or a hierarchy, but a network in which one can follow multiple routes and draw multiple, ramified conclusions. In my *Invisible Cities* every concept and value turn out to be double—even exactitude."[19] The construction of the many names of the city enables Calvino to keep these tensions at play. In the *Memos* he observes that the search for exactitude at work in *Invisible Cities* moves in two directions at once. On the one hand, exactitude moves toward "the reduction of secondary events to abstract patterns according to which one can carry out operations and demonstrate theorems; and on the other, the effort made by words to present the tangible aspect of things as precisely as possible."[20] As Calvino renders visible, through words, the many cities that he constructs, the word "city" remains a constant that enables connections and builds a bridge between Marco Polo and Kubla Khan. "City" is the image that allows Calvino to connect the many images of cities that he constructs: each has its own name, but they always have one name: "city." The name "city" and its many translations enable communication and build bridges thanks to which the invisible cities are given an image evoked by words:

> And yet I have constructed in my mind a model city from which all possible cities can be deduced," Kublai said. "It contains everything corresponding to the norm. Since the cities that exist diverge in varying degree from the norm, I need only foresee the exceptions to the norm and calculate the most probable combinations."
>
> "I have also thought of a model city from which I deduce all the others," Marco answered. "It is a city made of exceptions, exclusions, incongruities, contradictions. If such a city is the most improbable, by reducing the number of abnormal elements, we increase the probability that such a city exists. So I have only to subtract exceptions from my model, and in whatever direction I proceed, I will arrive at one of the cities, which, always as an exception, exist. But I cannot force my operation beyond a certain limit: I would achieve cities too probable to be real.[21]

Jammed Fields, Interstitial Debris

Under the name "city," we welcome those "magnetic field[s] jammed with objects" that Manfredo Tafuri had found in Giovanni Battista Piranesi's "invisible" city, the *Campo Marzio* (1761–62).[22] Tafuri had analyzed the dissolution of form performed by Piranesi in his etchings of prisons, the *Carceri* of 1760. But it is in the *Campo Marzio*, he observed, that the dissolution of form "touches urban structure . . . [it] touches both history, inasmuch as it is a principle of value and an instrument of action, and the very concept of the city."[23] For

Tafuri, Piranesi's *Campo Marzio* "is composed of a formless heap of fragments colliding one against the other."[24] It is "the "triumph of the fragment" dominated "by the formless tangle of the spurious organisms." And he continues, "Not by accident does it take on the appearance of a homogeneous magnetic field jammed with objects having nothing to do with each other."[25] But they do not "not have anything to do with each other": they collide, dissolve forms, and as fragments they have to reinvent their relations. What interests Tafuri here is that their clash "dissolves even the remotest memory of the city as a place of Form."[26] He sees the *Campo Marzio* as a "representation of an active decomposition . . . of the totality of Form,"[27] and this means of course not only the form of the architectural object but also of the form of the city. What next then?

While Tafuri was working on Piranesi, Colin Rowe presented his idea of a "collage city." But before collage, there is collision, which led Rowe to propose what he called "the politics of bricolage." "Collision city" includes both "closed compositions and *ad hoc* stuff in between." The model, for Rowe as well as for Piranesi, is Rome: "Seventeenth-century Rome, . . . that collision of palaces, *piazze* and villas . . . that inextricable fusion of imposition and accommodation, . . . an anthology of closed compositions and *ad hoc* stuff in-between."[28]

"So Rome," Rowe continues, "whether imperial or papal, hard or soft, is here offered as some sort of model which might be envisaged as alternative to the disastrous urbanism of social engineering and total design. Rome provide[s] perhaps the most graphic example of collusive fields and interstitial debris."[29] This is the moment that immediately precedes the collage; it is still fluid, it moves, but we still call it "city."

Mobile Words

Massimo Cacciari opens his essay *La città* (*The City*, 2004) with an analysis of Western history and the etymology of the word "city": "City does not exist, what exists are different and distinct forms of urban life. It is not by chance that "city" is named in different ways."[30] Cacciari observes that in Latin there is no equivalent to the Greek term *pólis*, and to the "ethnic root" of the *pólis* he opposes the "mobile concept" of *civitas*. *Pólis*, he explains, is the "place where a certain people '*gens/génos*' has its roots," and "one belongs to the *pólis* because there resides their *genos*."[31] "The *pólis* is ontologically and genealogically determined."[32] *Civitas*, instead, is "the product of the *cives* [a group of people] gathering together in the same place and organizing themselves with shared laws." *Civitas* is the convergence of people "*diversissime* (very diverse) for religion, ethnicity, etc. who *concordano* (agree) only by force of law."[33] "One becomes a citizen . . . because *si concorda* (one agrees) to obey those laws and to obey that regime: *concordia* [Lat.]."[34] The civitas is based on an agreement, a contract among the *diversissimi*: it is *hetero-geneous* (heterogeneous), open, and as such, it is open to the possible deviations of the *hetero-klitos* (heteroclite). Even Rome, the *Urbs*, the Ur-city—foundational, representative, symbolic, institutional, monumental, self-celebratory—is "founded on the agreement and the work of people who had been banned by their own city." It is "the place where exiles, wanderers, refugees, outlaws converge."[35] *Urbs* is not the city of "a defined group or race."[36] This "city is "mobile" in its very essence . . . *Roma mobilis* . . . [even] the extremely dynamic nature of the myth of its origin enables it to imagine itself and to construct its own myth through the synthesis of the most diverse elements . . . [and] what brings together these very different citizens is not their origin, but their common goal. [This] is the city projected towards the future."[37] "More than a foundational idea, the city is a foundational strategy: the city is thrust toward the future and in this [project] it brings together its citizens."[38] *Roma mobilis* is mobile in its origins, and is also a project for the future: "The goal here is the *imperium sine fine* (empire without boundaries) where, ultimately, the *orbis* becomes *urbs*."[39] "The fundamental programmatic character of the civitas is growth; . . . the city that always dilates, *de-lira* (*lyra* is the furrow, the mark that binds the city; one is 'de-lirious' when one trespasses the *lyra*, and exits the secure boundaries of the city)."[40] For Cacciari, it is important not to dismiss the city as the site of an unresolvable "acute contradiction," but to start from such a contradiction, to "value and explore it, and explode it."[41] Cacciari's interrogation of the history of the city continues. He looks at the process of dissolution of urban identity brought about by the metropolis, at the postmetropolis of the territory-city, and at the temporal rather than spatial relations of the deterritorialized territory. He then calls attention to bodies and places, and to a duty of form. He ultimately calls for beauty, in the sense of the Albertian *concinnitas* as syn-phony of the different, to rethink the city.

Still, we still call it city—or maybe not.

In 2003, the *Metapolis Dictionary of Advanced Architecture* edited by the Instituto Metápolis de Arquitectura Avanzada liquidated the word "city" with the following entry: "An old word. See 'm.city (or multicity)."[42] Around the same time, Saskia Sassen explained, less dismissively, "To more fully understand the impact of the digital and of globalization, we need . . . to suspend the category 'city.' Rather, we need to construct a more abstract category of centrality and of spaces of centrality, that, ironically, could allow us to recover the city, albeit a recovery as just one instantiation within a much broader set of issues."[43] Suspend, construct, recover the city . . . but within a much broader set of issues.

Laughter

In his discussion of the "composite character of beings" in "The Labyrinth" (1935–36), Georges Bataille uses the labyrinth, an image of incompleteness and intrinsic unknowability, to suggest that at the basis of human life lies "a *principle of insufficiency*."[44] It is insufficiency that determines a dynamic form of being, and questions the stability of human social forms. The reference to the labyrinth is important, because, while the labyrinth is one of the archetypal spaces at the origin of architecture, it is also characterized by mutable and experiential qualities. It is not a form that can be defined and known in its every detail. For Bataille the labyrinth is the image of the human being as a "being in relation,"[45] whose relationality is mediated by words and by the representations of existence that are constructed through language. Yet, "*knowing*— when a man knows his neighbor—is never anything but existence composed for an instant."[46]

Bataille extends the idea of the temporary and unstable nature of the connection between human beings from interpersonal relations to the much vaster and more complex network that is society. The "*knowledge* of human beings," he continues, "appears as a mode of biological connection, unstable but just as real as the connections between cells in tissue." Crucially, "the exchange between two human particles in fact possesses the faculty of surviving momentary separation."[47] Two important points derive from this. First, the connection between humans forming "unstable and entangled wholes" does not occur in isolation but within a "tissue"—it is a connection within connections. Second, this connection is not only momentary and labile but also productive of memory—it leaves traces that enable the acknowledgement and the recognition of a past, and therefore allows for both physical and temporal discontinuity. Being is precarious and negotiated, yet Bataille acknowledges the formation in this relational system of knots or concentrations, nuclei where "being hardens."[48] It is at this point that he shifts his argument from the idea of "being" to its multiple aggregations, to society, and to the city as its key form of expression. With the multiple aggregations of being, "relatively stable wholes are produced, whose center is a city, in its early form a corolla that encloses a double pistil of sovereign and god. In the case where many cities abdicate their central function in favor of a single city, an empire forms around a capital where sovereignty and the gods are concentrated; the gravitation around a center then degrades the existence of peripheral cities, where the organs that constituted the totality of being wilt."[49]

This is essentially a condensed account of the historical European city, but it is also the history of the superurban centralization produced and organized by nation-states. Bataille does not stop here but sets the whole process in motion, through cycles of constructions and destructions, organizations and their explosions: "Universality, at the summit, causes all existence to explode and decomposes it with violence."[50] As dynamic as Being, the City changes, and indeed it can be only if it changes. The change, far from smooth or gradual, is produced by the explosion of a discontinuity. Bataille illustrates this with the idea of "laughter." "Laughter intervenes in these value determinations of being as the expression of the circuit of movements of attraction across a human field. It manifests itself each time a change in level suddenly occurs: it characterizes all vacant lives as *ridiculous.* . . . But laughter is not only the composition of those it assembles into a unique convulsion; it most often decomposes without consequence, and sometimes with a virulence that is so pernicious that it even puts in question composition itself and the wholes across which it functions."[51] Laughter becomes the expression of a tension that activates societies and cities as dynamic fields, and manifests itself in paroxysms that produce both cohesion and discontinuity.

The dynamics of "laughing with" and "laughing at" establishes relations of association and opposition, produces condensations in groups, and constructs difference; but both types of laughter are always labile, volatile, and renegotiable. Laughter is contagious in both an associative and a dissociative way, and this idea enables Bataille to question the centrality of power and of the city by means of the very same forces that produce them.[52] The network of relations that organize social life is thus destabilized and set in motion, the center is emptied of meaning and of its controlling power, and the pyramidal social order is shaken. And so on, in a collective convulsion that destabilizes, making a city that is never complete and is constantly redefined in an open relation to others. Like language, the city puts us in relation to others, in ways that cannot be controlled.

Requiem?

In his collection of essays *Requiem: For the City at the End of the Millennium* (2010)—punctuation is crucial here—Sanford Kwinter seems to echo Bataille's idea when he defines the city as "a perpetually organizing field of forces in movement, each city a specific and unique combination of historical modalities in dynamic composition."[53] Toward the end of the volume, Kwinter concludes, "Although the city has disappeared, it is nevertheless here to stay—a clumsy paradox."[54]

By convention we name "city" those "center[s] of gravitation of beings" in which "relatively stable social groups" converge (Bataille). We continue to decline the word in innumerable versions, appropriations, adaptations, and reinventions in time and space. *In-exactitude* is necessary for the word "city" to be, as much as change is necessary in order for the city to be.

There can be no conclusion here as city continues to englobe the hetero*geneous*, the hetero*clite*, the unexpected, the impossible. We can only continue, with Beckett: "I'll never know . . . . in the silence you don't know, you must go on, I can't go on, I'll go on." This is not a requiem.

NOTES

1 Italo Calvino, "Exactitude," in *Six Memos for the Next Millennium* (New York: Vintage, 1993).

2 Giacomo Leopardi, *Zibaldone di pensieri*, ed. Francesco Flora, 2 vols. (Milan: Mondadori, 1937), 1:145, 1150, 1123–25. Quoted in Calvino, "Exactitude," in *Six Memos*, 59–60.

3 Robert Musil, *Der Mann ohne Eigenschaften* [The Man without Qualities], vol. 1, part 2, chap. 61; Rowolt edition, 1978, 1:246–47. Quoted and translated in Italo Calvino, "Exactitude," in *Six Memos, 64.*

4 Samuel Beckett, *The Unnamable* (London: Faber and Faber, 2010), 134.

5 Ibid., 1.

6 Steven Connor, preface to, Beckett, *Unnamable*, xi.

7 Ottorino Pianigiani, *Vocabolario etimologico della lingua italiana* (Rome: Società editrice Dante Alighieri, 1907 / La Spezia: Melita, 1991).

8 Italo Calvino, "Exactitude," in *Six Memos*, 55–80.

9 Calvino prepared what he called the "memos" for the Charles Eliot Norton Lectures he had been invited to deliver at Harvard University in 1985–86. The lectures were never delivered, as Calvino died in September 1985. He had written five of the "memos"—on lightness, quickness, exactitude, visibility, and multiplicity. The sixth one, on consistency, was never written. The extant five were published in 1988, in English as *Six Memos for the Next Millennium,* and in the original Italian as *Lezioni americane.*

10 Calvino, "Exactitude," 55.

11 Calvino, "Exactitude," 60, 80.

12 Roland Barthes, *The Neutral* (New York: Columbia University Press, 2005), 55. Calvino, "Exactitude," 65.

13 Barthes, *Neutral,* 131.

14 Ibid., 130.

15 Ibid.

16 Antoine-Chrysostome Quatremère de Quincy, "Type," in *Oppositions Reader*, ed. K. Michael Hayes (New York: Princeton Architectural Press, 1998), 617–20, quote from page 618; emphasis mine. The original essay is in the *Encyclopédie Méthodique,* "Architecture," vol. 3, pt. 2 (Paris, 1825).

17 Lieven De Boeck, "Typology," *Seven Sins of Urbanism,* 2002 installation of eight tables, seven of which contain an offset-printed certificate on paper with a silkscreen stamp, and one of which contains a map, certificates, A2 tables, ninety by one hundred by ten centimeters. De Boeck's seven "sins" propose a designed written critique of seven key terms of the modern tradition in architecture. "Typology" is one of the sins. See Teresa Stoppani,

T

"Seven Thoughts on a Sin (Typology)," in *Negation in Art and Architecture*, exh. cat. (Amsterdam: 66 East Centre for Urban Culture, 2005), 12–13.

18 Ibid.; Calvino, "Exactitude," 71.

19 Ibid., 71–72.

20 Ibid., 74.

21 Italo Calvino, *Invisible Cities*, trans. William Weaver (New York: Harcourt, Brace, 1974), 69.

22 Giovanni Battista Piranesi, *Ichnographia Campi Martii antiquae urbis*, 1350 x 1170 mm. From *Il Campo Marzio dell'Antica Roma, opera di G. B. Piranesi socio della reale società degli antiquari di Londra* (Rome: Piranesi, 1762).

23 Manfredo Tafuri, *The Sphere and the Labyrinth* (Cambridge MA: MIT Press, 1987), 33–34.

24 Ibid., 34.

25 Ibid., 35.

26 Ibid., 36.

27 Ibid.

28 Colin Rowe and Fred Koetter, *Collage City* (Cambridge, MA: MIT Press, 1978), 106.

29 Ibid., 107.

30 Massimo Cacciari, *La città* (Villa Verucchio, Italy: Pazzini, 2004), 7; translation mine, here and in the following passages.

31 Ibid., 7, 10.

32 Ibid., 8.

33 Ibid., 9.

34 Ibid.

35 Ibid., 9–10.

36 Ibid., 12.

37 Ibid., 13.

38 Ibid., 13–14.

39 Ibid., 14–15.

40 Ibid., 16.

41 Ibid., 26.

42 Manuel Gausa et al., eds., *The Metapolis Dictionary of Advanced Architecture: City, Technology, and Society in the Information Age* (Barcelona: Actar, 2003), 111. Sanford Kwinter, *Requiem: For the City at the End of the Millennium* (Barcelona: Actar, 2010).

43 Saskia Sassen, "Scale and Span in a Global Digital World," in *Anything*, ed. Cynthia C. Davidson (Cambridge, MA: MIT Press, 2001), 44–48, quote from page 48.

44 Georges Bataille, "The Labyrinth" (1935–36), in *Visions of Excess: Selected Writings, 1927–39*, trans. A. Stoekl (Minneapolis: University of Minnesota Press, 1985), 171–77, quote from page 172.

45 Ibid., 174.

46 Ibid.

47 Ibid.

48 Ibid., 175.

49 Ibid.

50 Ibid.

51 Ibid., 176.

52 "Through a necessary reversal, it [laughter] is sent back [. . .] from the periphery to the center, each time [. . .] the center in turn reveals an insufficiency comparable to that of the particles that orbit around it. [. . .] laughter traverses the human pyramid like a network of endless waves that renew themselves in all directions. This reverberated convulsion chokes, from one end to the other, the innumerable being of man." Bataille, "Labyrinth," 176–77.

53 Kwinter, *Requiem*, 58.

54 Ibid., 92.

A Postlude

Cynthia Davidson

Taking to heart Italo Calvino's concern for the precision of language, I prefer not to call these "words attached at the end" an epilogue.[1] This text may appear at the conclusion of this volume, in the traditional position of an afterword, but its genesis was in a conversation that took place on October 3, 2020. That conversation, late in the afternoon of a sunny New England fall Saturday, brought together all of the organizers of and speakers in the "Exactitude" conference, not in a room but in an online Zoom grid of faces that I was charged with animating. I felt a bit like an orchestra conductor staring at players who had spent the day demonstrating their respective instruments. Now I had to tease out their major- and minor-key harmonies in order to produce a coherent closing performance. Given that assignment, the after-words here can only be called a postlude. Not in the musical sense of an organ voluntary—though I think here of Charles-Marie Widor's *Toccata* (from *Symphony for Organ No. 5*), a complex and

FIGURE 10.1. "Exactitude" symposium, screen capture, October 3, 2020.

uplifting allegro piece of "exit" music[2]—but in the etymological sense, for the important root of "postlude" is the Latin *ludere,* "to play." So if the final conversation was an opportunity to play with the many ideas introduced in "Exactitude," then this writing cannot be a summation, and certainly not a future projection. It, too, is simply something played—if not still playing—afterward.[3]

There are seventeen definitions of the word "play" in *Merriam-Webster's Dictionary,* and numerous colloquialisms—"play by ear," "play with a full deck," "play with fire," and so forth—each with a different meaning and intention. "Exactitude," the conference, was a play on Calvino's essay "Exactitude," in *Six Memos for the Next Millennium,* itself a kind of play, since of the planned six memos, only five were written before Calvino's untimely death. When Calvino defines what he means by "exactitude" in writing, he makes a short list that includes three phrases of interest here: "a well-calculated plan," "memorable visual images," and "language as precise as possible." Similar phrasings have historically also appeared in the work of architects: the "free plan," the "digital image," the "classical language," for example. But the disciplinary relationships of "plan," "image," and "language" aren't literal; the words are always in play, always being recalibrated or repositioned to be more precise.

Back in the 1990s, when I was editing the architectural tabloid *ANY Magazine*, we produced an issue called "The Dimensions of Play: Ways of Thinking Architecture and the City." In his regular FFE (Far From Equilibrium) column, in this issue titled "Playing by Ear," theorist Sanford Kwinter writes that "play" is "a new question" that is "always about delivering up the new." He continues, "Play introduces an altogether different type of productivity . . . it allows us a contractual suspension of the gravity of need, frees us of our ingrained meanness, and gives us the room to posit hypotheses that will not undergo verification by witless referees. Only in play do we today find the lost universe of pure truth."[4]

I did not inquire of the "Exactitude" organizers, who were seeking new hypotheses for making architecture, whether play was one of their expectations for the conference. Simply by their posing a literary work as a framework for thinking about architectural practice, I assumed it was. And there were other clues. When Calvino describes two paths in his writing, for example, he introduces yet another word, one that has been associated with architecture since the Renaissance: that is, "space." His two "divergent paths of knowledge" are the "mental space of bodiless rationality, where one may trace lines that converge, projections, abstract forms, vectors of force," and "a space crammed with objects and attempts to create a verbal equivalent of that space by filling the page with words."[5] While these offer options between which he can switch back and forth, exactitude can never be fully attained, he writes, because "'natural' languages [the verbal] always say something *more* than formalized languages can," as they involve "noise that impinges on the essentiality of the information."[6] I would liken his concept of noise to the excess or unnecessary affects that might differentiate architecture from building, and, arguably, could veer toward the inexactness of character.

Anyone who writes a paper intended for both a conference and a book is also likely to switch back and forth between two paths. For a conference the participants write papers to be read aloud. For a book those papers are likely to be revised, because writing that is intended to be spoken, particularly within a certain timeframe, is usually not writing for reading. These revised papers are often then edited for their noiseless, but not voiceless, presentation. Voice—or authorship—is not silenced simply because there is no sound.

Voice comes from that "bodily rationality" and "space crammed with objects" that the writer attempts to capture with words on a page. At "Exactitude" there was also speech after writing in the unscripted Zoom conversation. Technically speaking, if not theatrically, this speech was a "wrap-up," like Shakespeare's famous epilogue in *Romeo and Juliet*: "For never was a story of more woe / Than this of Juliet and her Romeo."

Yes, the play's the thing (at least it was for Hamlet). So let me return to the "Dimensions of Play," this time to my own Dear Reader column, in which I wrote about Skytown, my sons' imaginary airport/railroad station/traffic jam, an ever-changing series of urban zones or conditions that occupied a corner of our New York apartment. I concluded the column, which more broadly considered zones of conscious and unconscious habitation, as follows: "Now more than ever, when we no longer really occupy the city or the house, when we occupy different zones of one seemingly infinite grid, it is necessary to rethink the between conditions of space and time, dark and light. Only then will it be possible, in these zones, to leave room for play."[7] In this between condition, opposing views can play with and off each other.

The grid I faced on October 3, some twenty-five years after I wrote about Skytown, was clearly a between condition, between real and virtual, but it did not seem to be infinite. It was confined to my desktop, each speaker neatly framed and vocally contained by the Zoom program that cancels out simultaneous voices. Under these circumstances, in which any dialectical condition is seemingly smoothed and flattened, fiery debate is not possible, only politeness. So to break the sound barrier, I asked Chris Benfey, a professor at Mount Holyoke College in South Hadley, Massachusetts, who had spoken about weathering, "How is the weather in South Hadley today?" To which he replied, he didn't know; he wasn't in South Hadley. (So much for confinement.) And the play was on.

Earlier in the day, Chris had cited a line from Oscar Wilde's play *The Importance of Being Earnest*: "Whenever people talk to me about the weather, I always feel quite certain that they mean something else."[8] And in a conference on exactitude, it did mean something else. Introducing the unpredictability of weather, despite the annual *Farmer's Almanac* forecast and the efforts of meteorologists to make more precise, science-based forecasts, was one way to crack open the idea of—even the demand for—precision in architecture. Like conversation, weathering, for all its unpredictability, produces newness and surprise. But the actual cloud that hung over "Exactitude" wasn't a stratus or a cumulus. It was the many invisible digital clouds that build up somewhere in data centers—or the more "precisely" named cloud campuses.

Cloud campuses, or more accurately, *a* cloud, is where most Zoom recordings are stored. In her conference presentation, Teresa Stoppani had compared the historical city, the living city, and laughter with the newly populated (pandemic) city of Zoom, where laughter is difficult to share (the sound barrier again). To challenge this postulate, I simply asked her, "What makes you laugh?"

Teresa, momentarily startled, began to laugh nervously and then to wrack her brain for the names of comedians. Nervous laughter is good. It's often unexpected and can lead to random, and productive, associations (more on this later). Playing the Zoom grid like a chessboard, I moved my pawn to Antoine Picon and asked, "What makes you laugh?" And he, perhaps having mentally answered my question to Teresa, immediately said, Buster Keaton. Later, someone else said Charlie Chaplin. And suddenly the idea of laughter, with its punchlines and inside jokes, pushed a crack into exactitude. Ironically, Keaton's and Chaplin's imitations of mechanization and its breakdown, for all their seeming chaos, were precisely choreographed to guarantee the audience's laughter. In *The Cameraman*, for example, Keaton, after dozens of ridiculous mishaps, succeeds in becoming a newsreel photographer with the use of a rudimentary and outdated movie camera and the help of a pet monkey. He simply, and creatively, makes do, besting the more advanced cameras and their sophisticated operators. (And yes, he wins the girl too.)

The humor in mechanical failure has faded over time, however, as the mechanical was replaced by the electronic, and then by the digital. (Once upon a time, I could repair the four-cylinder engine in my Toyota Corolla; today when I pop the hood of my car, I can only identify the container for the windshield washer fluid.) The invisibility of the digital is the specter of AI, another "cloud" that hung over "Exactitude," threatening a future reign of precision.[9] In what Francesca Hughes calls "the maximally unknowable material world" in which architecture—all of us—operate, AI seems like a "maximally determined paradigm." Is that paradigm exactitude? While artist Bruno Munari's hacking of the Xerox machine in the 1960s was creative interference with its operation, producing, as Alicia Imperiale discussed, new types of images, his play with a single machine did not cause a network of machines in offices around the world to start spewing out Munaris. How do you hack a paradigm?

Well into our conversation, Teresa Stoppani turned the tables and asked me a question. "Where are you taking us?" she said. The conversation had swirled from weather to conspiracy theories (which are highly precise, according to Thomas de Monchaux), from laughter to post-truth to Konrad Wachsmann's belief—as told by Mark Wigley—that the future exceeds what we can imagine (perhaps this is why some of us are leery of AI). I had no exact answer for Teresa, because the very purpose of "Exactitude," it seemed to me, was to crack it open and see what might be inside. Antoine Picon had a better answer: "The advantage of a conversation is that you don't always understand what's going on in the head of the person you're talking with. You build something together." Bingo.

The humorist David Sedaris, in his online MasterClass on humor writing, advises his "students" to "ask better questions" when they want to develop material for their writing. Those questions arise in conversation, in life. And at the heart of those questions is play. For, as Kwinter wrote, "play" itself is a question.

NOTES

1 According to *Merriam-Webster's Dictionary,* the Greek roots of "epilogue" essentially mean "words attached (at the end)."
2 To hear a performance of Widor's *Toccata,* see, for example, Ernst-Erich Stender at the organ at St. Mary's, Lübeck, Germany, YouTube, April 24, 2015, https://www.youtube.com/watch?v=9OU_HlRLq6A.
3 A video of this conversation can be seen at "UMass Department of Architecture Exactitude Symposium, Fall 2020 Round Table," February 23, 2021, University of Massachusetts Amherst, https://www.umass.edu/architecture/video/umass-department-architecture-exactitude-symposium-fall-2020-round-table.
4 Sanford Kwinter, "Playing by Ear," FFE, *ANY Magazine,* no. 12 (1995): 60.
5 Italo Calvino, *Six Memos for the Next Millennium* (Cambridge, MA: Harvard University Press, 1988), 74.

6 Ibid., 75.

7 Cynthia Davidson, "Dear Reader," *ANY Magazine,* no. 12 (1995): 5.

8 Oscar Wilde, *The Importance of Being Earnest*, act I. In context this reads:

> *Jack:* Charming day it has been, Miss Fairfax.
> *Gwendolen:* Pray don't talk to me about the weather, Mr. Worthing. Whenever people talk to me about the weather, I always feel quite certain that they mean something else. And that makes me so nervous.
> *Jack:* I do mean something else.

Wilde is also credited with saying "Conversation about the weather is the last refuge of the unimaginative." Today, given the reassessment of technology's relationship with nature due to climate change, Wilde could be proven wrong.

9 Though it wasn't discussed, building information modeling (BIM), the ever-expanding catalogue of parts for architecture, seems, for some, to preclude creativity when a penny-pinching developer is a factor. BIM is hackable.

Selected Readings

Bates, Stephen, and Jonathan Sergison. "Working with Tolerance." *ARQ: Architectural Research Quarterly,* no. 3 (1999): 220–34.

Cadwell, Michael. *Strange Details.* Cambridge, MA: MIT Press, 2007.

Calvino, Italo. *Six Memos for the Next Millennium.* Translated by Patrick Creagh. London: Vintage, 1996.

Carpo, Mario. *The Digital Turn in Architecture.* London: Wiley, 2012.

Carpo, Mario. *The Second Digital Turn: Design beyond Intelligence.* Cambridge, MA: MIT Press, 2017.

Clarke, Joseph, and Emma Jane Bloomfield. *Perspecta 46: Error. The Yale Architectural Journal.* Cambridge, MA: MIT Press, August 2013.

Eigen, Edward. *On Accident: Episodes in Architecture and Landscape.* Cambridge, MA: MIT Press, 2018.

Emmons, Paul. *Drawing Imagining Building: Embodiment in Architectural Design Practices.* London: Routledge, 2019.

Evans, Robin. *The Projective Cast: Architecture and Its Three Geometries.* Cambridge, MA: MIT Press, 2000.

Evans, Robin, *Translations from Drawings to Buildings and Other Essays*. Cambridge, MA: MIT Press, 1997.

Frascari, Marco. *Eleven Exercises in the Art of Architectural Drawing: Slow Food for the Architect's Imagination*. London: Routledge, 2011.

Frascari, Marco. "The Tell-the-Tale Detail." In *Theorizing a New Agenda for Architecture: An Anthology of Architectural Theory, 1965–1995,* edited by Kate Nesbit, 500–514. New York: Princeton Architectural Press, 1996.

Hughes, Francesca. *The Architecture of Error: Matter, Measure, and the Misadventure of Precision*. Cambridge, MA: MIT Press, 2014.

Leatherbarrow, David. *Topographical Stories: Studies in Landscape and Architecture*. Philadelphia: University of Pennsylvania Press, 2015.

Leatherbarrow, David, and Mohsen Mostafavi, *On Weathering: The Life of Buildings in Time*. Cambridge, MA: MIT Press, 1993.

McVicar, Mhairi. *Precision in Architecture: Certainty, Ambiguity, and Deviation*. London: Routledge, 2019.

Pérez-Gómez, Alberto, *Architecture and the Crisis of Modern Science*. Cambridge, MA: MIT Press, 1983.

Pérez-Gómez, Alberto, and Louise Pelletier. *Architectural Representation and the Perspective Hinge*. Cambridge, MA: MIT Press, 1997.

Picon, Antoine. *Digital Culture in Architecture*. Basel, Switzerland: Birkhäuser, 2010.

Sennett, Richard. *The Craftsman*. New Haven, CT: Yale University Press, 2008.

Spiro, Annette, ed. *The Working Drawing: The Architect's Tool*. Zurich, Switzerland: Park, 2014

Tafuri, Manfredo. *Theories and History of Architecture*. London: Granada, 1980.

Tigerman, Stanley. *Schlepping through Ambivalence: Essays on an American Architectural Condition*. Edited by Emmanuel Petit. New Haven, CT: Yale University Press, 2011.

Till, Jeremy. *Architecture Depends*. Cambridge, MA: MIT Press, 2009.

Vesely, Dalibor. *Architecture in the Age of Divided Representation: The Question of Creativity in the Shadow of Production*. Cambridge, MA: MIT Press, 2004.

Vuong, Ocean. *On Earth We're Briefly Gorgeous*. New York: Penguin, 2019.

Contributors

SUNIL BALD is associate dean and professor at the Yale School of Architecture, where he teaches design, visualization, and theory. Sunil is also a founding partner of the architecture and design firm studioSUMO. In 2015 SUMO was awarded the Annual Prize in Architecture from the American Academy of Arts and Letters. SUMO's work, which ranges from installations to institutional buildings, has been exhibited in the National Building Museum, MoMA, the Venice Biennale, the Field Museum, the GA Gallery, and the Urban Center. In addition to practice, Sunil has an enduring research interest in modernism, popular culture, and nation making in Brazil, for which he received fellowships from the Fulbright and Graham Foundations and published a series of articles. Sunil has an MArch from Columbia and a BA in biology from the University of California at Santa Cruz.

CHRISTOPHER BENFEY is Andrew W. Mellon Professor of English at Mount Holyoke College. He is the author of five highly regarded books about the American Gilded Age, including *The Double Life of Stephen Crane* (1992) and *A Summer of Hummingbirds,* which won both the 2009 Christian Gauss Award of Phi Beta Kappa and the Ambassador Book Award. Benfey is a frequent contributor to the *New York Review of Books* and the *New York Times Sunday Book Review.* He is a member of the American Academy of Arts and Sciences and has held fellowships from the Guggenheim Foundation and the National Endowment for the Humanities. In 2013 he won the Harold D. Vursell Memorial Award of the American Academy of Arts and Letters, which is given to a writer whose work merits recognition for the quality of its prose style.

CYNTHIA DAVIDSON is cofounder and executive director of the nonprofit Anyone Corporation, an architecture think tank in New York City, and editor of the international architecture journal *Log,* which she launched in 2003, and the former *ANY* magazine, an architecture theory tabloid (1993–2000). She is also responsible for more than forty books in print, including twenty-four books in the Anyone project's Writing Architecture series, published with MIT Press. She cocurated *The Architectural Imagination,* an exhibition of speculative projects for Detroit shown first in the US Pavilion at the 2016 Venice Architecture Biennale, and started the pop-up architecture gallery Anyspace in New York in 2017. Davidson also teaches writing in the Graduate Architecture and Urban Design program at Pratt Institute in Brooklyn and at Cornell University's College of Architecture, Art and Planning program in Manhattan. The American Academy of Arts and Letters recognized her work with its Architecture Award in 2014.

MICHAEL DAVIS is professor of art history and director of the Architectural Studies Program at Mount Holyoke College. His research centers on thirteenth- and fourteenth-century French architecture. His publications include studies of Notre-Dame, Paris between 1290 and 1350, the Royal Palace in Paris, the cathedral of Saint-Etienne, Limoges, and the papal church of Saint-Urbain, Troyes. Current projects are devoted to the cathedral of Clermont-Ferrand and the workshop of the master mason Jean Deschamps, as well as digital reconstructions of lost buildings in medieval Paris, such as the Franciscan convent of Ste.-Marie-Madeleine, the Collège de Navarre, and the Collège de Cluny.

THOMAS DE MONCHAUX is an adjunct assistant professor of architecture at Columbia University GSAPP, who contributed to *LOT-EK:*

OBJECTS + OPERATIONS, a recent monograph on the work of LOT-EK, with whom he is a longtime collaborator and contributor. His writing about design has appeared in the *New York Times* and the *New Yorker,* as well as in such journals as *Log* and *n+1,* where he is an architecture critic. Thomas has been a guest editor of the *SOM Journal,* a recipient of Graham Foundation and other awards, a past Bellazoug Memorial lecturer at Yale, and was the inaugural recipient of the Winterhouse Award for Design Writing and Criticism.

ERIC HÖWELER, AIA, is an architect, designer, and educator. He is associate professor in architecture at the Harvard Graduate School of Design and serves as thesis coordinator for the MArch program. Eric is cofounding principal of Höweler + Yoon, a research-driven studio of twenty-plus designers working between architecture, art, and media. H+Y's work is technologically and formally innovative and deeply informed by human experience and a sensitivity to tectonics. Höweler is the coauthor of *Expanded Practice* (Princeton Architectural Press 2009). He received a bachelor of architecture from Cornell University in 1994, and a master of architecture from Cornell University in 1996.

FRANCESCA HUGHES IS an architectural theorist and educator. Having taught both design studio and history and theory for almost three decades between the Architectural Association and the Bartlett School of Architecture, UCL, in London, she was head of school and professor of architecture at UTS Sydney from 2018 to 2020. Hughes has served as visiting professor at the Berlage TU Delft and KU Leuven (Brussels), and as external examiner in numerous schools internationally. She is editor of *The Architect: Reconstructing her Practice* (MIT Press, 1996) and author of *Drawings That Count* (AA Publications, 2012), *The Architecture of Error: Matter, Measure, and the Misadventures of Precision* (MIT Press, 2014), and, most recently, *Architectures of Prediction* (Ediciones ARQ, 2019). Her current work in progress, *The Architect's Computer: an Indiscrete History of the Universal Discrete Machine,* investigates architecture's historical relations to computation, memory storage and retrieval systems, the algorithm, and the calculation of new "truths."

ALICIA IMPERIALE is visiting associate professor of history and theory at Pratt Institute and a critic at the Yale University School of Architecture. She was a Cornell University, Society for the Humanities Fellow in 2016 and has taught at Università degli Studi Roma

Tre, Studi Umanistici, Columbia University, Temple University, and Parsons School of Design. Her scholarly work focuses on the impact of technology on art, architecture, representation, and fabrication in postwar Italian art and architecture and contemporary architecture. She is author of *New Flatness: Surface Tension in Digital Architecture;* "Seminal Space: Getting under the Digital Skin," in *Re:Skin;* "Stupid Little Automata" in *Architecture & Culture;* and "An Ineluctable Geometric Character: Luigi Moretti and a Prehistory of Parametric Architecture" in *Log: Observations on Architecture and the Contemporary City.* Her book projects underway include *Alternate Organics: The Aesthetics of Experimentation in Art, Technology, and Architecture in Postwar Italy* and *Machine Consequences: Origins of Output.*

LAURE KATSAROS is professor of French at Amherst College, where she is also affiliated with the program in Architectural Studies. She is the author of two books, *Un nouveau monde amoureux: Célibataires et prostituées au dix-neuvième siècle* (Galaade, 2010), and *New York–Paris: Whitman, Baudelaire, and the Hybrid City* (University of Michigan Press, 2012). In 2014, she received a New Directions fellowship from the Andrew W. Mellon Foundation that funded a year of study in the history and philosophy of design at the Harvard Graduate School of Design. Her new book, *Glass Houses: Charles Fourier and the Utopia of Collective Self-Surveillance,* is forthcoming in 2022.

PARI RIAHI is a registered architect and assistant professor at the University of Massachusetts Amherst in the Department of Architecture since 2016. Prior to joining UMass, she taught at RISD, MIT, and SUNY Buffalo. Pari completed her PhD at McGill University in 2010. Her first book, *Ars et Ingenium: The Embodiment of Imagination in Francesco di Giorgio Martini's Drawings* (Routledge, 2015), traces the historical inclusion of drawing as a component of architectural design. Her forthcoming book, *Architectural Drawing in the Post-Digital Era: Disjointed Continuity* (in-progress, Routledge, projected publication date 2023), tracks the propagation of digital media and its effect on architectural theory and practice. Pari's work has been published in the *Journal of Architecture, Journal of Architectural Education,* and *Journal of Interior Architecture and Adaptive Reuse.* She has held two solo exhibitions of her work titled *Rising Measures,* in Amherst and New York, and a group show in Hanover.

TERESA STOPPANI is an architect, architectural theorist, and critic based in London, where she lectures in history and theory studies at the Architectural Association School of Architecture. She studied architecture in Venice (MArch and Architetto, IUAV) and Florence (PhD arch&UD), and has taught architectural design and theory in Italy (IUAV Venice), Australia (UT Sydney, RMIT Melbourne), and the UK (Architectural Association, University of Greenwich, University of Brighton, Leeds Beckett University). Teresa's research interests are the relationship between architecture theory and the design process in the urban environment, and the influence on the specifically architectural of other spatial and critical practices. Her writings have been published internationally in edited volumes and academic journals. She is the author of *Paradigm Islands: Manhattan and Venice* (Routledge, 2010) and of *Unorthodox Ways to Think the City* (Routledge, 2019), and coeditor of *This Thing Called Theory* (Routledge, 2016). She is an editor of the *Journal of Architecture* (RIBA/Routledge) and the instigator of the international architecture research collective This Thing Called Theory.

ADA TOLLA AND GIUSEPPE LIGNANO are architects, cofounders, and principals of LOT-EK. They studied architecture in Naples, Italy, at the Università degli Studi Napoli Federico II and completed their postgraduate work in New York at Columbia University, GSAPP. In 1993 Ada and Giuseppe established LOT-EK, an award-winning studio that makes sustainable and soulful architecture through the transformation of industrial and infrastructural objects. We make the ordinary extraordinary. Our practice is experimental, ecological, and technological. LOT-EK's projects, across architecture and art, include commissions in the United States and abroad for major cultural institutions and museums such as MoMA, the Whitney Museum, the Guggenheim, and the MAXXI. LOT-EK's recent monograph, *O+O: OBJECTS + OPERATIONS,* was published by The Monacelli Press. Besides heading their practice, Ada and Giuseppe have been teaching at the graduate level for the past twenty years. They are professors at Columbia University's GSAPP and lecture at universities and cultural institutions worldwide.

MARK WIGLEY is a professor of architecture and dean emeritus at Columbia University. His books include *Passing through Architecture: The 10 Years of Gordon Matta-Clark* (Power Station of Art: 2019), *Cutting Matta-Clark: The Anarchitecture Investigation* (Lars Müller, 2018), *Are We Human? Notes on an Archaeology of Design* (written with Beatriz Colomina; Lars Müller, 2016), *Buckminster Fuller Inc.: Architecture in the Age of Radio* (Lars Müller, 2015), *Constant's New Babylon: The Hyper-Architecture of Desire* (010 Publishers, 1998), *White Walls,*

Designer Dresses: The Fashioning of Modern Architecture (MIT Press, 1995), and *Derrida's Haunt: The Architecture of Deconstruction* (MIT Press, 1993). He has curated exhibitions at the Museum of Modern Art, the Drawing Center, Columbia University, Witte de With Center for Contemporary Art, Het Nieuwe Instituut, and the Canadian Centre for Architecture. Most recently he curated *Passing through Architecture: The 10 Years of Gordon Matta-Clark* at the Power Station of Art, Shanghai (2019–20).

ALEJANDRO ZAERA-POLO is an architect. He trained at the Escuela Técnica Superior de Arquitectura de Madrid (hons), and at the Graduate School of Design, Harvard University (MARCHII with distinction). He worked at OMA in Rotterdam between 1991 and 1993, prior to establishing Foreign Office Architects in 1993, and AZPML in 2011. His work has consistently merged building practice with theoretical practice, integrating architecture, urban design, and landscape in his projects. His practice has produced critically acclaimed and award-winning projects for the public and private sector on an international scale. As a theorist he has published two books, *The Sniper's Log* and *The Ecologies of the Envelope* (Barcelona, Actar, 2012 and 2021), and has published extensively in professional publications such as *El Croquis, Quaderns, A+U, Arch+, Log, AD,* and *Harvard Design Magazine.* He was the inaugural director of the Seoul Architecture Biennale in 2017. Zaera-Polo was the dean of Princeton SoA and of the Berlage Institute in Rotterdam. He has taught at Yale University SoA, Columbia GSAPP, UCLA SoA, Yokohama University, and the Architectural Association.

Index

average, 40, 105, 139, 142, 144, 156n5,
157n10; and *homme moyen*, 143

Babbage, Charles, 38, 138, 144, 152, 154
Bannon, Steve, 35–37, 42
Barthes, Roland, 11, 163, 165–66; *The
Neutral*, 165
Bataille, Georges, 171–73; "The Labyrinth," 171, 175n52
beauty, 18–20, 22–23, 25, 30n22, 82,
153, 171
Beckett, Samuel, 11, 137, 154, 156n1,
159n41, 160n42, 160n44, 163–64,
173–74; *Three Novels: Molloy,
Malone Dies, The Unnamable*,
159n41, 160n42
Benjamin, Walter: "The Work of Art
in the Age of Mechanical Reproduction," 130
big data, 10, 42, 70, 137–40, 144, 148,
154, 156n2, 158n24
Bleam, Greg, 60
Bochner, Mel, 120, 126
body, 19; functions, 21, 25
Brecht, Bertolt, 37; Brechtian, 35
Buddha, 85, 98
building physics, 40, 43, 47
building systems, 27, 66

Cacciari, Massimo, 11, 163, 169–70; *La
città*, 169–70
CAD software, 118
Caillois, Roger, 122, 127; *Man, Play,
and Games*, 122, 132n11
calculation(s), 9, 15, 17–21, 25–26, 44,
80, 93, 109, 140, 143, 189
Calvino, Italo, 1, 2, 6, 11, 12n2, 78–79;
Invisible Cities, 79, 167–68; *Six
Memos for the Next Millennium*, 1,
2, 78–79, 84n9, 87–88, 112, 115–16,
162–68, 174n9, 178
Canguilhem, Georges, 141, 142; *The
Normal and the Pathological*,
156n5
caprice, 139, 141, 144; and causality,
148, 152, 153–55
carbon emissions, 34, 40–41
causality, 144, 148, 155

chance, 9, 26, 29, 122, 124, 126–27,
132n11, 132n18, 138, 141–43, 146,
154, 157n12, 158n24, 158n28, 169;
The Taming of Chance (Hacking),
157n12, 158n28
Chaplin, Charles, 181
chemical, 15, 38, 43, 46
Chirac, Jacques, 39
circumstance(s), 8, 90, 180
city, 10–11, 21, 41, 44, 48, 88–89, 109,
120, 162–63, 167–73, 179–80; historical city, living city, and the city
of Zoom, 181
classical architecture, 24
cleanliness, 23
climate change, 3, 6, 32, 36, 41–42, 46,
76–78, 83, 183n8; climatic conditions, 7; climatic crises, 6
Clinton, Bill, 35–36
code, 9, 109, 118
collaboration(s), 87, 91, 128, 162
collage, 169
collage city, 169–70
Collier, Sean, 7, 54–58, 64–65, 69
computation, 15, 17, 34, 126, 157n11
computer numerical control (CNC)
machines, 55, 117–18, 120, 131n3
conservative, 43–46, 49n7; conservatism, 47
constant (as invariable), 20, 112, 138,
140, 168
construction, 1, 3, 7, 18, 20–21, 34,
42–43, 48, 51–52, 54–55, 58, 64–66,
69–70, 90, 91, 93, 103, 117; drawing, 100
context(s), 3, 8, 9, 162
control, 5, 18, 23, 55, 59, 64, 69, 139–
40, 144, 154, 159n33
Conway, Kellyanne, 36
COVID-19, 6, 11, 32–35, 41, 43, 46,
156n2
craft, 2, 24–26, 28
creation, 2, 4, 11, 76–77, 119–20, 130,
133n25
creative, 6, 182; asymmetry, 46;
misuse, 8–9; potential, 123;
power, 2–3; practice, 5; process, 8;
tensions, 4